PLAN YOUR MONEY PATH

CREATE YOUR OWN FINANCIAL PLAN

BILL HINES

Wild Lake LLC

WILD LAKE LLC

eBook ISBN 979-8-9870796-6-9
Paperback ISBN 979-8-9870796-7-6
Hardcover ISBN 979-8-9870796-8-3

Book Cover by Bill Hines

First edition 2024

To my beautiful partner in time, my wife Lori.

ACKNOWLEDGEMENTS

YOU'RE SIMPLY THE BEST!

Thank you to Lori Hines, Jenn Mayberry, Brittany Murdoch, and Derek Hines for their feedback and help designing the cover.

Thank you to my mom, Carol Zaharuk, our family's head of finance back in my childhood. Watching you work that checkbook at the kitchen table was an early motivator in my life.

Thank you to my advance readers Alexandre Polozoff, Stuart Matthews, Charlie Stone, Chris Bulinkis, Louis Molino, Bob Wallace, Keys Botzum, Tom Alcott, Rick Eaton, Matt Giovanelli, and Wolfram Volpi.

Thank you to my Kickstarter project backers Anthea Sharp, Chris Bulinkis, Will Eaton, Louis Molino, Kate Donlon, Peter J McNamara, Stuart Weinstein, Denise Cote, Karel Zuiderveld, K. Grunwald, and John.

The quality of this book was greatly improved with your help. Part of you now lives within it, and you should be proud that you're helping so many families to lead better lives.

CONTENTS

FOREWORD

STUART MATTHEWS, FOUNDER, PRALANA

When I retired in 2009, our plan was to finish building a custom home inside a large airplane hangar in north Texas, then develop our mountain flying skills in our highly modified Piper Super Cub, and thereafter spend a good bit of each year flying, camping, and hiking in the backcountry of the American West. With a home built inside a hangar fortress, we could simply turn off the lights, lock the door and fly away for an indefinite amount of time anytime we wished. All good and no worries.

But it wasn't to be. As I was finishing the home, my wife's health took a turn for the worse and I became a caregiver. Her wings were clipped entirely, and my flying became limited to north Texas and hosting some great 4th of July parties at "the hangar." At about this time, I came across an article in Consumer Reports magazine about the best retirement calculators. I had already built my own Excel spreadsheet to convince myself I could safely retire, so I checked out the CR article with great interest. I had lots of free time to do whatever I wanted to do but was homebound, and I came away thinking I could easily build a better general-purpose

tool than any of those featured in that article and that it might
be fun to give it a go. I had no thoughts of a second career, but
it became an engrossing challenge to design, build, refine, and
market such a tool. It was far more difficult and time-consuming
than I ever could have imagined.

The challenge of continually seeking improvements and getting the tool recognized was fulfilling and satisfied my need for
mental stimulation and a creative outlet while I tended to my
caregiver role, and in the process, I became less self-centered and
much more motivated to help others. So, the journey began, first
as an Excel-based tool and much later, after partnering with the
highly talented and hard-working Charlie Stone, it evolved into the
web-based Pralana Online.

This is my personal example of the fact that we absolutely can-
not predict the future. Regardless, I strongly believe in having
a plan and modeling that plan mathematically so I can sleep at
night, but with the full understanding that I must adjust the plan
periodically as the future unfolds. A major factor in modeling
the future mathematically is the degree of fidelity with which
one attempts to do it. My philosophy is to incorporate educated
guesses and everything I think I know into the prediction and to
supplement that with an ability to study the long-term effects of
variations in the most unknowable parameters, such as healthcare
costs, life expectancy, rates of return, inflation, and government
policy. And to do side-by-side comparisons of different settings for
these unknowable parameters and different life choices. And easily
make updates and changes as life happens.

Over time, there can be wide variations in income and expenses,
in your investments and how they perform. There are also choices
to be made, such as where to send the kids to college, where to live,
whether to take a more rewarding but lower-paying job, when to

retire, whether you will work part-time during retirement or travel extensively, whether you will downsize (or upsize) your home at some point, when to take your Social Security benefits, exploring options to minimize your taxes, and so on.

And there are the what-ifs. If I die unexpectedly, will my family be okay financially? Do I need life insurance? If so, how much? What if the market takes a nosedive right after I retire? How will that affect our retirement plans? What if inflation takes off? What if we need long-term care sooner rather than later? It's mind-boggling because all these variations, choices and what ifs are interrelated, which is why I think you need a tool that models all the interactions and helps you make sense of the options.

Modeling multiple options of basic assumptions and virtually all types of income and expense streams, investment options and the associated taxes, and all the interactions, and then making sense of the results, has been the driving force behind Pralana Online. If I get an idea that I want to explore, or if I'm suddenly faced with an unexpected event that affects my plan, it's quick and easy to just set it up as a new scenario and check it out. I don't need an advisor; I can do it myself at a moment's notice, anytime, day or night. It's liberating to have a plan and to be able to assess the likely long-term outcomes, and to know that if this or that happens, I'll still be okay. So, I always have an up-to-date roadmap and it helps me sleep at night.

Stuart Matthews, Founder, Pralana

INTRODUCTION

HERE YOU ARE, IN THE RIGHT PLACE, AND EXACTLY WHERE YOU SHOULD BE!

Welcome to the start of the rest of your life—the one where you aren't wandering in the (financial) dark without a flashlight. The one where you have a clear roadmap to your financial future, and mathematical confidence that you and your family can have the life you dream of! This book contains thousands of dollars worth of professional financial planning advice, hints, tips, and hacks.

We do a poor job of teaching financial literacy in the United States. The status quo keeps you unaware of when you can stop working. It keeps that tax money rolling in while you spin on the hamster wheel through old age and sickness. In the past (and actually, present) investment or insurance pros use financial plans as a lead-in to expensive asset management services or complex, expensive, risky insurance products. Your financial plan isn't their focus and isn't where they make their money, so it doesn't get the ongoing care and feeding it needs. The plan is, often, "you need to buy my stuff to succeed." But, it's the most valuable thing for you and your family. Your plan may determine you're not quite there yet. Many struggling families will see this result at first. The silver lining is that it will tell you what you need to do to get there, and can guide you toward that dream.

The problem with the old way is, one weekend you and your spouse/partner might muse about retiring early, buying a vacation home, a boat/RV, or other dream over a glass of wine, and want to know if it's do-able. You then have to wait until Monday, try to contact your advisor, wait to get on their dance card, and likely pay mo' money. What a buzz kill! ***This book is the answer to those problems. It shows you how to take control and build your own financial plan, using high fidelity, inexpensive software, not the watered-down simplistic financial/retirement planning "tools" you find all over the internet.***

Why is asset management expensive? Most advisors charge 1% or more. At 1%, that's over $800 per month on a million-dollar portfolio. You don't write a check—that payment comes out of your investment profits, so you never see clearly what you're paying. On top of that, they may put you in expensive managed funds that earn them commission (which the fund pays, but they build the expense into your fees). They may gamble with your money, resulting in long, complex statements full of investments you don't understand and are robbing you of life lived. One percent doesn't sound like a lot, but the additive impact over years can rob you of a large percentage of what you would have had to enjoy otherwise. The sad part is that it's unnecessary. Advisors can't beat a simple, inexpensive index fund over the long haul, especially after factoring in their fees. There's nothing to manage in those index funds—they simply track the index (such as the S&P 500, or total US stock market).

Why are some insurance products complex, risky, and expensive? Because that's what keeps you dependent on them once you buy the sales pitch and product. The sales pitches are misleading, and the fees are often egregious. The contracts are often so long and complex that consumers give up trying to understand them, putting their faith in the misleading sales pitch. They are risky in that you are turning your money over, not "investing" it. You are buying a product; your money is gone for a promise. If the company goes belly-up or sells your policy to an offshore private equity firm (common these days) that doesn't have to follow stringent US regulations, you could be in trouble. The states have bailout help that *may* pay pennies on the dollar, but there's typically no bailout "funds," they simply try to find another insurer to pick up the policy.

This is true of annuities and complex permanent life insurance policies like indexed universal life (IUL). Will you really need to be paying thousands of dollars a month for life insurance in your old age? Of course, one could make the same argument of term life insurance, which is the good kind. Term policies are temporary and inexpensive, so there's less risk. Group policies through employers are a good way to buy term policies, and you can often add additional coverage during open enrollment. Be aware that if you leave the company and need to buy it on your own, it could be difficult if you have developed any pre-existing conditions.

Planning tools will help you determine if you need term life insurance to cover any exposures for your family. Our goal is to ensure you're self-insured—the best kind of insurance. It's a shame to see the insurance industry bending political arms to have these products made available inside worker retirement plans like 401ks. Simple annuities like Qualified Longevity Annuity Contracts (QLACs) and Single Premium Immediate Annuities (SPIAs), which start paying you in the short term, are better than ones where you expect to get the money well into the future. You still have to worry about whether your insurance company is viable and whether they'll sell your policy offshore.

> NOTE: I don't mean to demean everyone in the business. It's my profession, after all! If you prefer to have someone manage your assets and the math works, there are many investment advisors, financial planners, and insurance agents that are truly altruistic and take the fiduciary standard seriously. Their pricing is transparent, up-front, and no-nonsense. You'll know you've found one when you're told exactly what you're getting and what it will cost, with no run-around or need to listen to a long pitch first. No cheesy catch-phrases like, "When you do better, we do better!" Always vet them at FINRA Brokercheck [1]. Search on both the advisor's name and the company name. Look at their ADV form, which says how they make their money in sections 4 and 5. Look for any disclosures on the site and in the ADV, because that's where anything they may have done wrong in the past is documented. If you're a high net worth person or family or have a complex financial situation, you may get value from that professional expertise.

I'm a professional investment advisor, financial planner, and financial counselor. There are no sales, gimmicks, or hooks in this book. If you want to use the planning tool I demonstrate, you'll have to buy it. It's inexpensive and I have no financial relationship with their excellent team. This book's mantra is financial simplicity and having as few people (and contracts!) between you and your

---

1. https://brokercheck.finra.org/

money as possible. It's time to take control of your financial life, and I hope to illuminate the path for you.

This book will first take you through some general financial planning context, and then take you through the steps to building a financial plan for a sample family. Along the way, we'll discuss the different inputs and assumptions required for any financial plan, as well as how to interpret the results and put your plan into action. This is not a user manual for that tool. I won't go into every obscure nook and cranny of Pralana, because it would get boring and those side areas aren't relevant to most people. This book is more of a casual, informative walk through how to use the tool to set up a financial roadmap for the average household, using an average household as our example. It is how I would guide you, as a client, to learning and using the tool for your own benefit. I won't spend a few hundred pages telling you, "Click here. Type this." OMG, that would be tedious. I'd much rather take you through the great Dick and Jane sample, page by page, discussing the inputs, analysis, and results with all the hints, tips, and insights I can conjure up.

I'll minimize the use of screenshots, as they're quickly outdated and a detriment to those who need to or prefer to listen to audiobooks. I won't use them for pages with just a few simple inputs. It will also help to apply this book to high-fidelity financial planning tools other than the one I will use in this book. Screen shot are a conundrum, because the graphs use color, but it's prohibitively expensive to use color in a book. They're also detailed and it's hard to see that detail in a physical book (you can pinch and zoom in the eBook, of course). So, as a compromise, I'll put the high-resolution full-color graphs in a PDF that will be free in my Pralana Retirement Calculator User's forum on Facebook, or by request by emailing me at bill@wildlakellc.com. Hopefully, you'll be using the tool, and will see the ones specific to you!

This is a book about creating your own financial plan, using a sample representative family and reviewing their configuration, optimization, and analysis. We cover the most commonly used settings, inputs, and assumptions. The user manual is now built-in to the tool, context sensitive, comprehensive, and awesome, so please defer to it to clarify or add to anything in this book that you don't fully understand, as well as the extremely helpful user forum at the Pralana website[2].

> NOTE: Some knowledge of personal finance topics is necessary to do planning. I provide context where I can, but can't go into the nuances as the book would quickly become unwieldy. I cover those topics in detail in my prior book, *Kiss Your Money Hello (and Financial Stress Goodbye)* [3]. I don't want this to come off as an upsell by mentioning that to excess throughout this book. So please be aware that book is available in case you need the refresher on those topics. If you find yourself unable to do this with confidence, head to the Advice Only Network [4] and other resources mentioned above.

PS About that cover... I wanted something to symbolize our life path and financial journey. The trees represent those major

---

2. https://pralanaretirementcalculator.com

3. https://books2read.com/kissyourmoneyhello

4. https://www.adviceonlynetwork.com/

goals in our lives. Money is scattered along the path to represent how it helps us to achieve those goals. Our money path continues even after we pass, typically with some type of estate left behind (which we'll cover). That's why the image on the book cover doesn't end. If you look closely, the figure is poised at a beacon leading upward, to whatever comes after, hopefully, a life well lived. And that's why *you* need a plan. *Let's go build it together.*

PSS If I could ask one thing—if you enjoy this book, please leave a rating or review at your favorite book site. It's hard to get visibility without them. Welcome aboard!

Bill Hines, Emancipare.com

CHAPTER ONE

WHAT'S A MONEY PATH AND WHY DO I NEED ONE?

IT'S A FINANCIAL ROADMAP FOR THE REST OF YOUR LIFE!

Questions, We All Have So Many Questions!

WHAT GOES THROUGH OUR minds when we lie awake at night after a hard day at work? Some of these questions might sound familiar.

- *Will I have to work until I die?*

- *Will the people I leave behind be OK after I'm gone?*

- *When can I stop going to this job I detest?*

- *When exactly can I retire?*

- *Can I quit or take a sabbatical and maybe go travel*

the country in an RV?

- *Can I afford to send my kids to college, tech, or trade school?*

- *Will I go bankrupt and lose my home and cars if I get laid off?*

- *Can I have my dream (early/FIRE?) retirement?*

- *Will I have enough money for long-term care that's not in a rat-infested dump?*

- *Should I do Roth conversions?*

- *Should I create a charitable trust?*

- *How should I invest?*

- *How can I pay the least taxes over the rest of my life?*

These are the questions that keep folks up late at night, or quibbling among themselves. A money path answers those and many more. I often call it a financial roadmap, because it lays out the money moves you should make over the rest of your life. It's a living plan you can (and should!) update or what-if to your heart's delight.

NOTE: Throughout this book, I will use the terms money path, financial plan, and financial roadmap interchangeably. They're the same thing. I dislike the term retirement plan, because this is a plan for everything financial over the course of the life, not the end of it! A true money path will consider money for your kids' education, your future homes and cars, relocations, jobs, side hustles, and so much more, not just retirement. You should have a financial plan early in your adult working years, so it evolves with you and your goals over your life.

I talked about the "old" days when you could only get a true, high-fidelity financial plan by submitting yourself to professional advisors or insurance people. There weren't any high-fidelity consumer facing tools available. There were only simple tools that were nowhere near the fidelity needed to answer your questions with precision. If you use tools that do things like optimize your Social Security strategy, taxes, or Roth conversions, be aware that they are operating in a vacuum. The math around these decisions is highly context-dependent and can only be done correctly when calculated as part of your overall financial picture and plans. Please don't make big decisions based solely on what they tell you!

Those days have now changed. Don't get me wrong—there are still a bunch of really sad, misleading financial planning tools out there. The good news is that there are actually a couple of high-fidelity, inexpensive, consumer-available products that you can trust to build your own money path. With a plan in place, you can simply pull it up over that glass of wine and ask whether the math still works if you decide to retire early, move to Hawaii, and buy that boat. You get the idea. It's a magical thing! We'll discuss a few options and pick one to guide you through building your very own plan as we go through this book.

Many people have realized they don't need an investment advisor to manage their assets. The cat's out of the bag. Personal finance bloggers with big megaphones and vast audiences drive this point home regularly. Heck, if you know when you plan to retire, or when you need that college 529 plan money, you can simply pull up a Vanguard target date fund for around that year and see exactly how the best pros in the business think you should invest your money! And, guess what you'll see—the same simple three to four fund portfolio of index-fund ETFs I and many other altruistic financial writers advocate for. It's not black magic, and the vast and growing population of DIY investors, Bogleheads, FIRE (Financial Independence/Retire Early) advocates have figured it out.

I showed you an easy trick (inspecting Vanguard target date funds) to get an idea of how you might invest your money, avoiding tons of fees. Hey, we're only in chapter one and this book has already paid for itself countless times over! There are some other variables to consider, such as your personal tolerance for risk and volatility. I cover risk tolerance with clients, and you should factor it in as well, for both you and your spouse or partner. If you're a person who gets very nervous when the stock market or economy isn't doing well, you can ask a good planning tool if it's OK to put less in stocks and more in safe fixed income. Don't take more risk than you need to, it's bad for your sleep.

The investing part isn't all that complicated, given what we've just covered. Building a financial plan is a whole other thing! Investing is just one factor in a comprehensive, robust, trustworthy financial plan. Other components to be factored in are things like health care, long-term care, Social Security, Roth conversions, charitable giving, taxes, and more. You need to know a bit about those things in order to build your financial roadmap.

Most professionals won't build a plan for you unless you agree to let them manage your investments. We've already ruled that one out, for most people. So, what if you're comfortable managing your own investments but not quite enough to build your own financial plan? There are folks out there that will guide you through it, or build it for you the first time, and teach you how to take the wheel from there. Look for advice-only financial planners on websites like adviceonlynetwork.com, or hang around the social media sites and discussion forums for your favorite tool. Read up, search, and ask questions.

I mentioned that a financial plan is a living document. It doesn't take much care and feeding. Once you've done your base plan, you can note any near-term to-do items, put them on your calendar, and put it away (other than those what-if dream sessions over a glass of wine!). You will want to update it at least once a year, typically in early January, with an updated copy of your preferred software, so that you have the latest tax tables, features, and other updates. Investment management and financial planning don't take a lot of housekeeping! And once you've done the work, enjoy more restful nights and more harmonious relationships.

Why Do I Need a Money Path?

To relieve money stress! To solve the great mysteries of the rest of your life! More simply, to answer the questions we started this chapter with, and many more, any time you want. To not end up working at Walmart in your elder years, unless, of course, that's what gives you happiness. Without a true financial roadmap, you are wandering through your life, financially, in the dark without a flashlight. Those lights at the end of the tunnel could be an oncoming train. Yeah, that's stressful, or it should be.

- You might be a young person, vowing to be financially independent, so you never have to spend a day of your life at a job you dislike.

- You might be a 50-something, just finishing up paying for your kids' education, and realizing you don't have a plan for your own retirement.

- You might be retired or about to retire, and unable to enjoy the joy of this time in your life because of uncertainty.

Everyone needs a plan. When faced with bad news, such as an impending layoff or health scare, you can ease your pain by jumping in and gaming things out. The joy in my work has always been those clients who come to me saying, "I know I'll work until I die." Typically, after we do the math and use the software to optimize and save on taxes and other strategic moves, they're presented with the mathematical confidence they can retire far sooner than they ever envisioned. And, with a far better quality of life—more vacations and leisure activities! That's a life well lived.

Listen, you work hard. By this point, many of you have worked hard for a very long time. You may have raised your kids by now, which is certainly hard work. You deserve the best. Let's make a plan to make sure you get it. Which brings me to my most important point.

We live in a society that's uber-competitive, excessively greedy, and over-driven in terms of the push to drive harder, do better, over achieve. It's one thing that's made America exceptional. Of late, however, the scales have tipped against the average worker. CEO pay was around 20 times the average worker's pay throughout the "good old days," the 1950s to 1970s, when a single bread-winner could support a middle-class family. Now it's several hundred times more. Back then, someone with just a high school education at a manual labor/factory job could buy a modest home, decent car, and afford to have their spouse or partner stay home if they wished to, and retire in dignity with a pension. Work hours were pretty strictly 9am to 5pm, with a nice full lunch hour and a few weeks of vacation. I know, because that's what my family was like when I was a child. I remember it was far less stressful.

All that has changed, just in the space of a generation. My parents had that life, and it was gone by the time I started a family. It's never been a thing for most of you, unless you're older than me, which is hard to beat. What I see in my clients are people who are emotionally (and often physically) spent, even the younger ones. It's not a hamster wheel anymore, it's a robotic assembly line that spits out worn parts and moves on to a newer model of a younger, energetic human cog. Don't even get me started in what I see in the older clients. It sickens and saddens me until I show them they can quit today. I'm always sad for the ones that don't find me, or haven't created a plan on their own.

Commercials and social media also pit us against one another, to keep up with the Jones', in a game that everyone loses. The status quo drives us to spend and spend, borrow and borrow. Those things are antithetical to a stress free, happy life, financial independence, or early retirement. Worse yet, we get stressed by these factors; we worry it'll be worse for our kids (spoiler alert: it probably will be) and we drive them to achieve, achieve, achieve. That was my thinking when I was a young dad. I wish I knew all this back then. Planning is the recipe for not having to work as hard. Part of planning is to make sure you can leave the legacy you desire to your heirs.

A plan frees you from this stressful uncertainty. It allows you to devise your escape route, even if you're not there yet. It allows you to see what's needed to get there and sets those milestones in clear view for you. It shows you the way to peace and safety. We envy other cultures for their laid-back approach to work and life, their long vacations and lunch times and short work days. Planning can do that for you. It certainly empowers you, and it feels different going to the job when you're financially independent. If you get laid off, you can afford to take a nice sabbatical and maybe retrain to a new vocation before re-entering the workforce. Maybe set up and open a small business. Your plan will tell you whether it works.

Do you want further motivation? Explore these three very revealing "life" questions (called the Kinder Questions). It helps to understand more about yourself and helps you identify all your goals in life. If you have a spouse or partner, do it together. They work in sequence, so don't move on to one until you've finished the one before it.

1. Imagine that you are financially secure and that you have all the money you need for the rest of your life. How would you live your life? Would you change anything? Don't hold yourself back, let yourself go! Don't hold back your dreams.

2. This time, you visit your doctor, who tells you that you have five to ten years left to live. The good part is that you won't ever be sick. The bad news is that you will have no notice of the moment of your death. What will you do in the time you have remaining?

3. This time, your doctor shocks you with the news that you have only one day left to live. Notice what feelings arise as you confront your very real mortality. Reflecting on your life, on all your accomplishments, as well as on all the things that will remain

undone, ask yourself, "What did I miss? Who did I not get to be? What did I not get to do?"

Sobering, isn't it? Keep those answers handy. You'll need them as you map out your lifetime money path as we go through this book!

The Planning Process

The planning process typically proceeds in several phases, as follows.

Build. This is where you tell the tool about your current assets, income, expenses, family, plans for the future, and assumptions. It's a lot of data gathering, but once you're done, it's all in one place. For example, you may have to set up an account at ssa.gov in order to get your Social Security Primary Insurance Amount (PIA) at your Full Retirement Age (FRA). Remember those acronyms, they'll be important later in the book when we cover your income!

Review. Double check those numbers in the tool to ensure they're all correct, and nothing critical is missing. Garbage in equals garbage out, after all.

Analyze. This is where you set the tool loose to run Monte Carlo and/or historical simulations to determine whether your goals are realistic and achievable with a reasonable confidence of success (i.e. not going broke in your old age). We usually shoot for 90+% success, but some folks are more flexible, and we'll get into all that later.

Optimize, rinse and repeat. If the tool says you're not quite there, we then turn to optimizations and other tactics to get a better result. If it says 100% success, well, actually, that's good, but not optimal. You're working too long, or maybe not spending enough in retirement, or both! A high-fidelity tool will allow you to ask both questions. "Ok, smarty algorithm, when is the earliest I can retire with a 90+% chance of success?" Or, "Exactly how much more can I spend each year and still stay above the golden 90%?"

What-If? Once you have your base plan established, you can do side-by-side what-if analysis for any alternate scenarios you can dream up, such as relocating to another state, retiring even earlier, living longer, buying a vacation home/boat/RV and so much more.

Periodic review. You should pay attention to any new releases or bug fixes for your tool, and re-run your model when those appear, just to be sure they don't affect your plan. As well, update your plan early each year with your new start-of-year account balances, new version of the tool (with updated tax tables), and any changes to your personal situation or goals.

A Word About Simplicity vs Complexity

You may have seen all the cool click-bait articles and posts on social media about hacking your personal finances. These offer tactics like:

- Using a different asset allocation (stocks vs. bonds) in your different asset locations (brokerage, Roth, pretax)

- Going 100% equities/stocks in your Roth account because the growth is tax free

- Taking money out of your pretax accounts prior to eligibility and paying the penalties

- Taking loans out of your workplace retirement plans

- Buying permanent/whole-life insurance or annuities

(careful there, the sales pitches are very misleading!)

Keep in mind, techniques like this **might** "optimize every dollar." However, as with many tactics in personal finance, it's not just about math. Weigh other non-mathematical factors. For example, claiming Social Security early because of poor health or a family tree not tending toward longevity, or doing Roth conversions at higher tax rates to protect a spouse against widow/widower single tax rates if one of you dies prematurely.

If you use financial planning or investing tools, you may find the overall benefit of tactics like this may be quite small for your own personal situation. Given that, why not just take the simple approach and allocate your asset locations the same? What is the return on your investment (ROI) for adding this complexity? Is it worth it? The benefits here are that a non-financial driven spouse/partner can easily understand and manage, should you become incapacitated or die, rather than have to submit themselves to the predators out there. It allows them to be in the loop with the easy management/housekeeping (yearly rebalancing, managing glide path). It protects you from yourself as you age and are more likely to make very expensive mistakes. It's less work, meaning more time for other things you should enjoy in life and retirement.

NOTE: In my years as a financial planner, when I've had DIY clients who are neurotically obsessed with "every dollar" optimizations like those I just covered, after their plan is done I find most often they come nowhere near spending the money in their lifetimes, even counting what they want to leave behind. Is it worth obsessing to that degree if your plan is fully funded and more?

So, what tools do we use to get there? Let's have a look.

CHAPTER TWO

MONEY PATH STRATEGIES AND TOOLS

THEY'RE HIGH DEF, LOW DEF, GOOD, BAD, AND UGLY

Money Path Strategies

IF YOU READ FINANCIAL content, or if the internet notices that you're interested, you know there are endless strategies to have a successful financial life and retirement. Some are old, some are new. Some might work for the intended audience, but you may not be aware you're not in that demographic and pursue them to your detriment. Let's explore a few.

Dividend Strategy

Some folks use a dividend strategy where they have all dividend and interest payments diverted to their checking account to live on in retirement. They try to never sell their shares or bonds, considering them the "cash cows" that give milk. It's an old-school strategy that I don't recommend. We've seen recently that during recessions or other hard times, companies can and will cut dividend payments. Interest payments are quite variable and are all over the map in recent years. You want as much consistency and predictability as possible in retirement.

4% Rule Strategy

The 4% Rule is a very simple and popular retirement strategy. It results from a study that was done (called the Trinity Study) in the 1990s to answer the question, "What is a safe amount to withdraw from my nest egg in retirement, so I don't run out of money?" Spoiler alert! The answer is 4% per year, increased annually for inflation. So, for example, if you have a million dollars saved, you can take $40,000 in year one. If inflation that year was 3%, the following year you'd take out $40,000 times 1.03, which is $41,200. This keeps your purchasing power intact. There are some caveats, however. It is based on the assumptions that your nest egg is reasonably allocated between stocks and fixed income (somewhere between 60/40 and 50/50), has low fees, and your retirement will last *thirty years or less*.

NOTE: The FIRE crowd, who seek to retire earlier and younger than traditional retirees, should be cautious, as their time horizon will probably be longer than thirty years. This also goes for the common FIRE advice (FIRE number) of having 25 times your expenses, which is just the same math as the 4% rule put differently.

It's interesting that during the twelve-year bull market run prior to COVID, people following the 4% rule saw their money piling up. This led to speculation that perhaps it should be the "4.5% rule" or "5% rule" (Barron's recently put out an article saying this). Then, in the recession following COVID, you saw talk that it should be the "3.5% rule." I found that hilarious. Humans! It's important to note that the math in the original study does account for up and down economic circumstances, so that stuff is all baked in already.

The 4% rule is simple and easy, but perhaps too simplistic because it assumes you'll want or need the same amount of spending power in each of the thirty years of your retirement, i.e. from age 65 to 95. Most folks want to spend more in their early, healthy, go-go phase of retirement, and won't be capable of spending that much when they're in the very slow no-go phase late in life. It leads to nice inheritances for those left behind, but is a lot of life unlived for retirees.

Bucket Strategy

The bucket strategy is a simple way to view and manage your nest egg withdrawals. You picture your money in three virtual buckets. Bucket One has the nest egg money you'll need for the next two years of retirement. That money should be in safe, insured high-yield savings or money market accounts. Bucket Two should have the following three years of money needed from your nest egg. Those funds should be in safe, higher yielding US Treasury bonds or other bond funds. Bucket Three would be the rest, and in stocks/equities with dividends reinvested.

In December of each year, you set up monthly automatic transfers from the Bucket One account(s) to your checking. This is just like a monthly paycheck, like when you were working. At the end of year one, Bucket One is, of course, half empty. It needs to be refilled! Where do you get the money from? Well, if looking back, the stock market has had a good year, Bucket Three is probably overflowing. Take those winnings off the table, sell some, and fill Bucket One back up. If the stock market was down, bonds (especially US Treasuries) should be up, so refill by selling bonds in Bucket Two. There are very rare occasions where both stocks and bonds are down in the same year (2022 is one of those). In that case, do nothing. That's why you have two years of cash in Bucket One! There's a good video of this strategy by Christine Benz of Morningstar [1] on YouTube.

In reality, as Michael Kitces (a preeminent financial blogger) has written about[2], this exercise is really akin to rebalancing your portfolio each year. You also have to juxtapose these buckets against your preferred asset allocation! If you have a high net worth in financial assets, doing the buckets could lead to an aggressive stock/bond allocation of 90/10. In that case, one idea is to fill Bucket Three with a mix of stocks and aggregate bond funds to get to the preferred asset allocation. Aggregate bond funds yield more than safer US Treasuries because they hold corporate bonds, real estate and mortgage-backed securities. On the flip side, if you have low financial assets, Bucket One and Two may hold almost all your money, leading to a very conservative asset allocation such as 10/90, which may not have enough growth to sustain your

---

1. https://www.youtube.com/watch?v=ycRE4DBFnEc

2. https://www.kitces.com/blog/are-retirement-bucket-strateg ies-an-asset-allocation-mirage/

retirement (remember, the 4% rule specifies somewhere between 60/40 and 50/50).

> TIP: Be careful about aggregate bond funds, especially in a taxable brokerage account. There is more trading churn in these funds than funds that only contain US Treasuries, hence there are rebalancing costs that are difficult to track or anticipate with planning tools.

FIRE (Financial Independence/Retire Early)

The FIRE movement started some years ago, fueled by Generation X and Millennials who questioned the status quo of working most of their lives just to get their "freedom" about the same time they have health and other aging problems. The concept is to be minimalist, save, invest wisely, and be able to retire early or at least be financially independent. For most, the emphasis is more on the financial independence part. It sure feels different going to work when you know you don't need to be there financially. It makes things like sabbaticals possible. Most of the folks who have followed this path "retire" in their 40s or 50s simply move to starting a small business and monetizing their passions. It's not work if it's fun, right?

I'm a fan of simplicity, but I've always been concerned when reading FIRE articles or blogs about the penchant to oversimplify things. Advocates use simple formulas like having a "FIRE number" of twenty-five times your expenses in order to determine you're good to go. That recipe is flawed because it's based on the 4% rule, which is based on a thirty-year retirement. If you FIRE at 45 years old, you've likely got a much longer timeline, and could find yourself working as a big box store sample handout person at 85 years of age (unless that's your passion). It's also flawed because, as we'll see, your expenses will change dramatically over your life. If you're retiring before 65, you need to figure out health care. If you're retiring before 59 1/2, you need to make sure you can get by without touching your pretax accounts, or you'll be paying penalties. I love everything about FIRE except the FIRE bloggers that make *their* money by hawking credit cards and point/mile schemes on their followers, some of whom may have had problems using credit in the past. Nobody gets wealthy by abusing credit cards, and the point/mile rewards get more restrictive by the day.

On the flip side, I always worry when I'm working with a young couple that says they plan to work until late in life, because they love their careers and jobs. A lot can happen, and will. Team Evil can replace that wonderful management team in a heartbeat. The company can be bought out or go out of business. They may decide they no longer need your services after you start to age and slow down. Kids may come into the picture and you realize you'd prefer to be spending more time with them. And certainly grandkids! Have a plan, be independent.

Other Strategies

There are endless variants of the safe withdrawal rate question. The term itself is incorrect in a sense—it should be called the safe spending rate, not the safe withdrawal rate. If you withdraw the money but don't spend it, you're good to go! Some spending strategies are tied to economic metrics like the CAPE ratio. A good, high-fidelity financial planning tool will tell you exactly how much you can spend per year. Better yet, you tell the tool what your dream retirement looks like, with your spending in various life phases, and it tells you whether the math works. That said, I'll detail a few tools specific to this topic in the next section.

Money Path Tools

Let's get one thing clear from the start. Your spreadsheet sucks. I know it's your baby. You've been cultivating it, feeding and caring, for many years, and you're very proud of it. I know because I've looked at many that clients have devised on their own. Even the better ones were not even close to a high-fidelity tool. But, kudos for taking a nice shot and the old college try. I should qualify that. The only person whose spreadsheet doesn't suck is Stuart Matthews (see the foreword). Nice job there, Stuart!

Any tool that offers to give you complex information, such as when you're financially independent or can retire, and only asks you to answer a few simple questions, isn't useful. Sorry, it's just not that easy. A money path is like a grand mosaic of pieces that all interact and affect one another. Have you taken Social Security earlier? You may have just made your Roth conversion path a lot more expensive because of higher taxes. You may have to pay back your health care subsidies. That's why you need one comprehensive high fidelity tool to rule them all, not a piecemeal approach of different things that work independently of each other.

The other problem with these high-level rules of thumb are that they assume consistent spending throughout the rest of your life. You will typically have four phases of life and spending:

1. *Currently working*

2. *Early/young retirees, the "go-go phase" when you're active, healthy, energetic and eager to hit your bucket travel list and engage in active recreational*

activities.

3. *Beginning of aging, perhaps in your 70s, when you move to a "slow-go" phase, maybe not as much active sports like kayaking or hiking.*

4. *Your latter years, in your 80s, the "no-go" years when you're not anxious to travel, perhaps eat less and stay home more. And, to not be an ageist, not everyone is the same! I recently went to see Neil Young and Crazy Horse, a band of rockers at/near their 80s. They blew the roof off the dump and wore me out. Therefore, you need a plan that's specific to <u>you</u>.*

You might even add a phase for when your kids' education spending is done and you have an empty nest. That's why you should lay out your spending in phases, planning to spend more in those early go-go retirement years and less in the later years. It's a key non-mathematical factor in when to claim Social Security, which we'll cover later. The desire to do more earlier, while you're healthier, is a key reason those high-level metrics that assume consistent spending throughout your life are flawed. That's why you need a high-fidelity plan.

Some tools are merely fronts to capture your data and upsell you, so be careful. We're talking about long-range planning tools here, to map your financial path for the rest of your life. So, you really don't need a tool that is connecting to all your accounts and sucking in your personal data 24/7. Some of you are likely privacy-oriented, and don't want your sensitive financial data out there in the cloud somewhere. A high-fidelity tool doesn't need

your passwords, account numbers, or even your last name to do
its work. As you'll see, you're essentially telling it what kind of
accounts your money is in (brokerage, Roth, 401k, IRA, 529,
HSA...), how much is in each place, how it's invested (at a high
level), how much you're making and contributing (if you still are),
what your plans are (man plans, God laughs). These tools churn
through economic scenarios based on past data (usually back to
1928, some as early as the 1800s) and give you an idea what chance
of success you have. Success is measured by being able to achieve
your stated goals, and a reasonable assurance of never running out
of money.

The tools will typically offer both Monte Carlo and historical
simulations. In the former, your assumptions (or the defaults)
about asset classes (stock, bond, cash, you can add your own)
returns are randomly varied and bounded by their standard deviations to simulate good, moderate, and bad returns over time. Historical simulations will take actual economic trends dating back to
1928 (before the Great Depression) and see how you'd fare in those
sorts of circumstances by using actual asset returns and inflation
from those periods of time. Both are useful, and we'll discuss why
as we get into it!

We should never be overconfident. Who knows what's
next—alien landing, world war, pandemics, climate disasters. If
you use historical simulations, a good era to pick is the actual
worst ever time to retire. Amazingly, it's not the eve of the Great
Depression. It was the long-running recession starting around
1965, which featured sky-high interest rates, high inflation, high
unemployment. If your planning tool offers both historical and
Monte Carlo simulations, it's not a bad idea to have a look at both.

> NOTE: The primary enemies of long-term financial plans are higher than expected inflation and sequence risk. On the former, we always have inflation. Prices almost always go up, as do wages. But ***unexpectedly*** high inflation can wreck a financial plan. There are ways to mitigate that, and we'll explore them. On the latter, sequence risk means that the "sequence of events" that happen leading up to when you need to start using your nest egg are bad. For example, the day after your kid starts college or the day after you retire, the market crashes and you are overly exposed to stocks. You can't ride it out and forced to sell devalued shares. We can fix that too. Stay tuned!

We usually shoot for 90% success rate or better. Why not 100%? If times get tough and we have a long-running recession, most people will tighten their belt a little out of normal human behavior. Perhaps take one less vacation a year until things rebound. That natural human behavior will often over-compensate for the single-digit chance of failure and keep you on the right course. But, if you're someone that has no restraint and will spend with abandon no matter what, shoot for 100%! It's not uncommon for people to want to be super-conservative at the start of their retirement. It can be intimidating stepping into that brave new world!

A good tool will have things like a Roth conversion optimizer, nest egg withdrawal optimizer (to show the best place to draw money from each year), Social Security optimizer, a When Is My Earliest Safe Retirement Date feature, and a How Much More Can I Spend Safely feature. It should allow you to lay out your expected spending in different phases of your life and allow for several side-by-side what-if scenarios and modeling. It should provide you with a clear, year-by-year roadmap for the rest of your life. It should provide details—never rely on some high-level assurance like, "Your chance of success is 95%!" Dig into those details to verify the results. It's important to know where the money is coming from each year to fund your expenses.

Here are some options I feel are worth mentioning:

- **BigERN** at the earlyretirementnow.com site has done an exhaustive study with many blog posts and some tools to explore many safe withdrawal strategies, such as tying your withdrawal rate to financial metrics like the CAPE ratio. But this isn't a true comprehensive financial plan.

- **cFIRESim** at cfiresim.com is aimed at the FIRE audience and is free, and a medium-fidelity web-based calculator.

- **Fidelity Retirement Planner** at fidelity.com is a web-based free, consumer-facing limited version of the advisor/planner tool eMoney (which is owned by Fidelity). It's high-fidelity and pretty good, but will probably get you some nags to use Fidelity's professional services. If you already have all your money at Fidelity, you may feel more at ease with this tool—they already know everything about your money. If you don't, you can add outside accounts to your profile.

- **Boldin (formerly New Retirement) PlannerPlus** at b oldin.com is a web-based high-fidelity financial planning tool, and there is a much lower fidelity free version. The paid version (Planner Plus) is comprehensive and very graphical. They recently renamed it to Boldin. That concerns me, because when I see a well-named tool renamed to something agnostic, it usually means they're going to branch out to try to be all things to all people, and that usually doesn't go well.

- **Pralana Online** at pralanaretirementcalculator.com is an inexpensive web-based high-fidelity financial planning tool. Its legacy is as a desktop application written on top of Microsoft Excel (hence, my reference to the creator, Stuart Matthews, at the start of this chapter). Its major benefit has always been keeping your data private (on your own computer), in case you are privacy-centric. The new online version stores your inputs on their servers, but you don't need to use your last names and it requires no account linking, account numbers, or other sensitive info, other than your birth dates. You have free access to backup and delete your data. The user manual (PDF and online) is superb, as is the user discussion forum on the website. Please use both resources as companions to this book. Between all three, your questions should be answered quickly and correctly.

If you'd prefer not to do it yourself, other options are to use Vanguard Personal Advisors. They will manage your portfolio and help with some planning/withdrawal issues for a pretty low fee. They will do a financial plan, but not a comprehensive one. NerdWallet is also reportedly getting into the advice-only game and providing some type of financial plan. Boldin has advisors as part of its network. I'm a fan of finding an advice-only planner who will take the time to build a relationship, tutor/mentor you, and use a tool that you can also use. If that's your jam, you might start looking here adviceonlynetwork.com. There is a curated list of consumer-facing financial planning tools and other great articles, reviews, and resources at caniretireyet.com. It's worth noting that there are no free high-fidelity consumer-facing financial planning tools (other than the Fidelity one, if you're a customer), but the above are certainly affordable. If used correctly (what this book is all about!), the benefit is usually immense.

By now you're wondering which are my favorites? Let's be transparent and cut to the chase! To me, Pralana Online is a clear #1, followed by Boldin PlannerPlus, followed by the Fidelity tool. Those are the only high-fidelity planning tools I'm familiar enough with to recommend, or would based on what I know about the ecosphere of tools. As I said earlier, these three are very similar in how they work, because they're doing a very similar thing. That's good news.

For the balance of this book, I'm going to use Pralana Online to show you how to create your own money path. I've been using the Gold/Excel version for years and find the new Online version has too many enhancements and improvements to ignore. As well, the computing is shifted into the cloud and off my aging laptop, so it's much faster. That's how we'll roll in this book, but if you're using something else, the discussion and techniques involved should apply. Financial planning tools all require the same inputs!

Let's get started!

CHAPTER THREE

GET STARTED DOWN YOUR MONEY PATH

FOLLOW THE YELLOW BUCKS ROAD!

BEFORE YOU EVEN PUT pen to paper (I guess it's fingers to keys these days...) let's pause a moment. Find some time to think and reflect on what you're trying to accomplish. If you're a young person or couple, that might involve simply sketching out a rough roadmap of what you want out of life. If you're an older person or couple contemplating retirement, you might dream about what that retirement looks like. It's a wonderful exercise to do in those quiet non-distracted times when you can have a proper conversation with yourself or partner in life. It's kind of hard to do it as well when you're sitting in front of a computer dealing with a bunch of numbers. Don't hold back. I see too many clients that are so desperate to make the plan work they leave out the things they really dream about. You've worked too hard for that. Shoot for your best life, and we'll see if you need to come back to Earth a little later on.

A few things to consider:

- **How old do you think you'll live to?**

- **How many kids (if you're young)?**

- **Will you change locations? To where and when? Buy or rent a home?**

- **Any expensive toys on the radar (boat, RV) or a vacation home?**

- **How much, if anything, do you want to leave behind—property vs "Whatever is left" vs a discrete amount?**

- **When would you like to retire or become financially independent? What will you do with your time?**

Knowing the answers to questions like this, at least preliminarily, can make the planning process go more smoothly. Planning tools are good at math. But this isn't just about math. This is about happiness! The goal is to live life on your terms, doing what makes you happy every day. It's important to keep that in mind when making decisions along the planning path. The Social Security optimizer may tell you mathematically it's best to wait until age 70 to claim. But what if you have significant health problems, or a family lineage that doesn't lend itself to longevity? What if it means you have to go to that job you hate, every day for another five years, just to get a bump in your SS payment, at an age when you may not enjoy it as much?

Planning tools show the clear deltas of these choices. You can see the monetary difference in taking Social Security payments earlier vs. later and decide. For example, if your payment is $2,000/month at age 62, and you wait five years to age 67, that's $120,000 of life unlived left on the table. That's a lot of go-go age fun, or else it could be banked and invested. The break-even point in waiting is often in the mid-80s. The decision, of course, is more complicated and depends on a lot of other context, as we'll see. This is all about making informed choices about your future.

> TIP: As a compromise, it's a common tactic to have the spouse with the Social Security higher benefit wait and let the benefit grow, while the spouse with the lower benefit claims early. We'll see later how to optimize Social Security and accept the optimized date, or plug your own in manually.

OK, I've procrastinated and blathered on enough, and your fingers are itchy. Let's get to it! As stated, I'll walk you through the process of creating your money path in the Pralana Online planning tool, but you may use one of the other products I've mentioned and follow along.

Here we go. I'm going to walk you through the Dick and Jane Pralana sample, because it's a good one. It represents an average family. Don't worry, I'll add tips and hints for folks who might be single, different ages than Dick and Jane, and other deltas. If you want to learn Pralana by building a sample plan, just follow along with me and enter the same information I describe. Or, use the descriptions, hints, and tips to enter your own. I've altered Dick and Jane a bit to make a few important points. I'll make the plan available for you at the Pralana Retirement Calculator Users group on Facebook, if you prefer. Be aware that if you load it, it will overlay anything you've entered already!

Meet Dick and Jane! The sample family are a married couple in their mid-40s with two teenagers. They live in California but would like to retire in their early 60s and move to Texas, after the last of their kids goes to college. They are very much statistically average in terms of their income and savings. Isn't it discouraging when you read examples about people that have all the money? Dick and Jane are regular folks.

My Family and Children

The home page of Pralana Online shows the Build, Review, Analyze, and More menu links across the top banner. Position at the Build→Get Started→My Family page (as noted by the breadcrumb menu at the top). If not, you can get there by choosing Build→My Family from the top menu. Most planning tools will start by asking basic information, as Pralana does. However, don't be tempted to choose Quick Start. That's a lower-fidelity shortcut, and we don't take no stinking shortcuts around these parts, pardner! (However, a low-fidelity shortcut is still better than no plan at all...)

	Advisors ▼	Build ▼	Review ▼	Analyze ▼	Mo
Get Started		**Financial Assets**	**Income**	**Expenses**	
Quick Start		Management	Employment	Personal Property	
My Family		Account Initial Balances	Pension	Rental Property	
Scenario Assumptions		Simple Portfolio Modeling	Social Security	Children	
Import PRC Excel Export File		Advanced Portfolio Modeling	Windfall	Healthcare	
		Scheduled Withdrawals	Annuities	Long-Term Care	
		SEPPs	Other Income	Term Life Insurance	
		Personal Loans		Cash Value Life Insurance	
		Investment Loans		Charity	
				Phased	
				Miscellaneous	

Pralana Build Menu

Dick and Jane have chosen Married in the marital status drop-down and typed in 2024 as the year their plan starts. I've never used or seen anyone else use a different year than the current year and not sure why you would. They have entered their birth dates of 5/15/1976 and 7/13/1978 and the tool has calculated their age at the start of the plan year (Jan 1). Don't be confused if this isn't your current age, as your birthday may have already occurred this year. We see that Dick and Jane are 47 and 45 years old, respectively.

> TIP: Living together but not married? This is a problem for financial planning. I'm not aware of a tool that handles this situation accurately. So, there's a decision to make. You can combine your info in one family plan and choose married as your status. There's not an enormous difference in state/federal income tax sometimes, but it could throw off things like Social Security spousal benefits. You'd have to do some math to offset that and add the additional tax, for example. A tool like https://tpc-marriage-calculator.urban.org/can be helpful. You could also just make sure your plan is more conservative in other ways, to leave enough wiggle room it doesn't make a difference. The other choice would be to create two separate plans, as single, and figure out what percentage of expenses each of you will pay.

Most financial calculators like to start at the beginning of the year, even if it's already late in the year. Don't worry about that, you're just getting started, so it's OK. It's common practice to update the plan every January with your new start-of-year balances and other updates, so if it's late in the year, you're not too far away from that exercise.

> TIP: Don't be tempted to enter a different birth date for security. Your actual date of birth is very important in many of the calculations the tool will do. I never enter last names, nor do I ever use account numbers or any other "revealing" information. If you want to be Dick and Jane, go for it. I'm sure they won't mind!

The next field is Plan Description, which is the name for your plan. Mine shows "Dick and Jane Retire and Have Fun," or even use your last initial. You should notice that Scenario 1 is underlined at the top. You can use up to three what-if scenarios, and we'll talk more about that soon.

The bottom part of this page is where you tell the tool about any kids in the family. Dick and Jane's children, John and Sue, were born in 2008 and 2010, respectively. We have checked the box to indicate both are tax dependents. There are red x marks to delete children (oh, my!) and a row below to add more children.

Scenario Assumptions

Let's move on to the next item in the Build→Get Started menu and choose Scenario Assumptions. We discussed earlier how planning tools typically require three general sets of information—your current status, your assumptions, and your goals/plans for the future. Let's work on those assumptions. I'll use a subheading for each of the tabs on this page, so you can follow along.

Add/Delete Scenarios

Here it defaults to the label "Your Plan" for Scenario 1, but I typically use "Base Plan" to get the baseline down prior to doing additional what-ifs. Don't get tempted to start additional scenarios until you get your baseline well established. When the time comes, you may use them for things like a vacation home purchase, retiring earlier/later, or more optimistic or pessimistic assumptions.

> TIP: Pralana uses the term "baseline plan," when doing analysis, to reflect on what you had before making changes. I used to call my Scenario 1 "Baseline Plan" but that can cause confusion with the Pralana terminology on those pages, so I suggest "Base Plan," or perhaps even better, "Likely Plan." Use the notes field to put in details of what you're trying to accomplish with each scenario.

Retirement & Life Expectancy

Dick's planned retirement date is 12/31/2039 (age 63) and Jill's is 12/31/2042 (age 64). So, Dick will hang out at the country club for three years while Jill trudges off to work? What's up with that, Dick? I digress. It's not all that uncommon. Sometimes, one spouse has to continue on longer because of pension or employee stock plans vesting. Those are called "golden handcuffs" for a good reason! Using a high-fidelity planning tool, you may reveal the fact that you don't need them, and can shed those bonds (not the financial asset kind). If you're already retired, just put December 31 of the previous year.

TIP: It's a good time to remind you that you must have a plan for your time in retirement. I've seen countless examples of getting folks to that promised land, and having them come back and say, "I'm bored, I'm going back to work!" Often, we dislike going to our jobs so much, we're eager to get away, but then miss the daily social interaction and sense of self-worth. Think about volunteering [1] or starting up a small business to monetize your passions. The tax benefits can be great!

Now we get to the morbid part. We have to project how long you'll live. Ugh. The average life expectancy in the US is currently around 79 years, which is a pretty meaningless statistic. People are living much longer these days! It turns out that the longer you live, the more likely it is that you'll live longer than the average life expectancy. Planners and professional tools like to default to age 90. You'll see this kind of thing often—take the best guesses out there and then make them a bit more conservative. Of course, for you personally, this may very well be lower or higher based on your own health situation and family lineage. There are calculators that can help you get a better idea on the Social Security page[2], Longevity Illustrator[3], and death-clock.org. We never know when

---

1. https://www.marketwatch.com/story/the-volunteer-rate-among-retirees-is-depressingly-low-heres-how-to-change-that-71a3e97d

2. https://www.ssa.gov/OACT/population/longevity.html

3. https://www.longevityillustrator.org

our time is up, so it's good to test what will happen if one or the other spouse/partner passes early as part of our what-if scenarios, as well as what happens if you both live to a ripe old age of 100. Longevity risk in retirement is the risk that you'll live longer than you anticipate, and possibly run out of money.

In our example, Dick has estimated age 85 and Jane has estimated age 90, perhaps as pay-back for having had to work a few years after Dick has retired! Hopefully, she spends it at the country club.

Inflation

That mortality exercise was a bummer. Let's move on to the Inflation tab, which can be yet another bummer to think about! You'll see the ability to place different general inflation rates in different intervals. For example, you may be tempted to put a high interest rate for the next year or two if inflation is predicted to be high, and then use the long-term predicted rate following that. I'm not a fan of that strategy. We're using a long-term calculator to plan the rest of your financial life. I prefer to use the predicted long-term rate and allow the tool to work its magic. Historical analysis will use varying inflation rates, so you're covered there, as we'll discuss later. Don't get too carried away trying to predict the future, you'll always be wrong.

So, what might that inflation number be? I pay attention to what the top economists at Morningstar, the US government, and the big brokerages are forecasting. The thirty-year outlook is usually somewhere between 2.6-2.8%, so I use 3% in order to be conservative. Healthcare and long-term care costs go up more, so I normally put 2% for each of those (this is additive, in addition to what you put for the general rate). I add 1% for college costs, which, on top of the 3% I used for general, makes that 4% used in the calculations. There are fields to enter expected changes to Medicare premiums and IRMAA income limits, but again, I'm not a huge fan of trying to predict the future.

> TIP: Don't be tempted to put the same additive inflation rate for healthcare (2% in our example) for Medicare IRMAA Income Limits. Those are pegged to general inflation, so leaving this blank accomplishes that (unless for some reason you expect them to be more or less). An example might be if you hear rumblings about Congress making changes in order to shore up Medicare funding.

Residence/Relocation

That wasn't so bad, was it? Let's move on to the Residence/Relocation tab. Dick and Jane are currently living in California, but intend to move to Texas in 2041 when Dick retires. This section has fields to add alternate state tax rates and local income taxes, if your current or any intended future states of residence use those. For example, in Pennsylvania, localities can impose their own local income tax on top of the commonwealth and federal income taxes. This is an important tab for folks that intend to move to less expensive or more attractive climates (or both!) at any point in their lives.

If you're not absolutely sure about these future moves, you may decide to leave them blank and use them for later scenarios. There are several excellent websites for finding ideal locations to live (per your specific criteria!) such as Area Vibes[4], Best Places[5], City-Data[6], and Livability[7]. That was fun, thinking about future greener pastures (unless you're moving to the desert or snow...)! Now it's time to traverse another bummer fork down our money path—that of taxes.

Tax Assumptions

At the top of this page, you can model your own predictions about future federal tax rates. If you have that crystal ball, I'm dying to meet you! It's easy to be pessimistic here, and yes, taxes will just about always go up. But, I don't recommend trying to model that here. Maybe save it for a pessimistic scenario. The bottom part of the page is important. This is where you show whether you believe the Tax Cuts and Jobs Act of 2017 will expire (meaning the federal tax brackets go back to where they were previous to the legislation) or be extended. It's very hard for politicians to raise taxes even if that happens by doing nothing, as is the case here. In fact, in the past, it's been a pretty reliable way for them to get voted out in the next election cycle. That said, I prefer to take the conservative approach here as well, and assume it will expire as of 2026, as it is currently scheduled to. If that doesn't happen, it's gravy on your

---

4. https://www.areavibes.com/

5. https://www.bestplaces.net/

6. https://www.city-data.com/

7. https://livability.com/

plan! We'll know soon enough, and you can make the change then if you're wrong.

> TIP: We'll discuss Roth conversions later, but anticipation of this legislation ending, and tax rates going up, is driving folks to be more aggressive with that tactic up through the end of 2025.

FICA Assumptions

Move to the final tab in this section, which is FICA Assumptions. FICA is a Social Security payroll tax. As with the previous tab, you can model increases in FICA. I have the same advice here—unless you have it on very reliable authority that this will happen, I'd leave it out or save it for your pessimistic doomsday scenario. I know, we hear all the click-bait disaster stories about Social Security and the trust fund. It's the same political suicide we discussed earlier to let this system fail, and it's in better shape than most folks think. There will have to be changes, but they will probably affect younger workers who haven't been paying in for decades. If that's you, maybe use this for a pessimistic scenario. If you want to model perceived future drops in Social Security benefits, you can do that when we start to cover your income.

This wraps up our discussion on the Build→Get Started section! Let's move on to cover your financial assets.

CHAPTER FOUR

FILL IN YOUR FINANCIAL ASSETS

DEALIN' WITH THE DEETS!

Dick and Jane's Portfolio

IN THIS SECTION, WE'LL be doing some financial/investing math, so we'll need to know a bit about how Dick and Jane have invested their money. Let's assume they like to keep things simple, and since their retirement is in the early 2040s, they've had a look at Vanguard's 2040 Target Date Retirement Fund (Stock Symbol: VFORX).

You usually see this fund (or similar ones) as an option in retirement accounts such as traditional IRAs, or 401k/403b/457b plans. You could actually invest in this same fund in all your accounts, including your brokerage. However, I don't recommend that. If you choose a set it and forget it type fund like this (because of having a long stretch to retirement) you'd want to sell it as you approach your goal and then invest the proceeds similarly to how the fund is set up. The reason is so you have flexibility—for example, as you need the money, in years when the stock market is down you can simply sell shares of the bond funds, and vice versa. Holding only the target date fund, you don't have that flexibility. You can only sell shares of the target date fund, which means selling a mix of stocks and bonds.

This is a problem in a taxable brokerage account—you'd have to sell the target date shares and then immediately realize all the gain in the share price. It could lead to a big tax bill just as you're at peak career earnings and tax brackets just as you retire. So, in the taxable brokerage at least, you'd want to not buy the target date fund, but set up your portfolio similar to how the target date fund is invested, even if you won't need it or quite some time.

I use Vanguard's funds quite a bit for examples, because the expense ratios are very low, and therefore don't need to be "factored out" of much of the math, especially if you are simply replicating those funds by investing in the same ETFs in your own portfolio.

VFORX at this writing is 77% stocks and 23% fixed income. It's simply built, with just four inexpensive index funds! Here's what it looks like at this writing:

- 47% in Vanguard's total US stock market index fund (VTI)

- 30% in Vanguard's total international stock index fund (developed countries outside the US only, VXUS)

- 16% in Vanguard's US aggregate bond fund (BND)

- 7% in Vanguard's international aggregate bond fund (BNDX)

Vanguard uses aggregate bond funds. These hold highly rated corporate bonds (no junk bonds), real estate funds, mortgage-backed securities, etc. For that reason, they yield more than boring old US Treasuries. It's a strategy when there's a long time horizon to the goal. However, as always, with more reward comes more risk! See the tip in Chapter 2 about the sneaky tax problems you may incur with these.

Because these aggregate bond funds hold corporate bonds, they can track, or correlate, a bit similar to the stock market (but with far less volatility!). When people lose confidence in stocks, they sell, and they also sell corporate bonds. Risk averse folks, especially those nearing or in retirement, may prefer to take their risk in the equity portion of their portfolio, and keep the fixed income part more steady, boring, and aren't correlated to the stock market. This means when they hear the stock market is down, they usually will see their fixed income portion is going up, and that feels a bit more reassuring. This happens here because when people are scared and selling stocks, they often run for the safety of US Treasuries, causing them to rise. The same could be said about gold and other safe harbors, but they don't pay interest or dividends.

As well, higher than expected inflation can be a threat to retirement, so it's not uncommon to set a healthy portion of the fixed income piece to inflation-protected US Treasury bonds (commonly called TIPS). You often see Vanguard add these into their target date funds as retirees approach their target date. After the sky-high inflation of 2022, more investors are going with these as part of their strategy. Expected (normal) inflation is already priced into bonds and bond funds. Inflation protected bonds and bond funds are for higher than expected inflation. As usual, you are transferring risk, and there is a slight payment due to that in terms of expense. Be aware that if you hold TIPS in your taxable brokerage, they will generate taxable income through basis adjustment for inflation as well as interest.

> TIP: Building bond ladders by purchasing individual bonds is a popular approach. But, it means ongoing work to maintain the ladder, and if you need the money prior to maturity, selling the bonds at auction—the Treasury won't buy them back. Bond funds are much simpler, and some call them the ultimate bond ladder. While bond fund dividends are actually interest taxed as regular income like individual bonds are, when you sell the shares (if you've held them longer than a year) they're taxed at the often preferable long-term capital gains rate.

You will often see tax optimization tips such as, "put all your fixed income in your pretax/IRA accounts, and all your equities in your taxable brokerage account, and make your Roth 100% equities because of the tax free growth." For normal folks, there's not really much of an advantage here, but if you're a high net worth person, this could be worth the extra complexity. Knowing how beneficial to you specifically these strategies are is a benefit of having a plan! You can game it out by using a high-precision tool like Pralana.

For most folks, I often find it sounds good on paper, but it's not worth the hassle. Deciding on your optimal asset allocation and making it the same across all your asset locations (taxable brokerage, pretax, Roth, etc) has benefits in simplicity, supervision, and management. Don't forget—mistakes are very expensive, and the more complex your investments are, the more housekeeping they require, the more likely you will make mistakes, especially as you age. And as well, what if the financial driver in the family unexpectedly passes away? The surviving spouse will be much more able to take the wheel and not be thrown to the predatory wolves I talk about in the beginning of this book. And having the Roth at 100% equities can be dangerous if the market drops precipitously just as you need the money. Complexity often makes money for other people on your dime. Simple for the win. More time for fun stuff! If you're planning on leaving that Roth behind to someone who won't need the money for a while, sure, go for it if you'd like.

Retirement is all about living every day on your terms and doing what you enjoy—being happy! If nerding out on bond ladders and asset location strategies butters your bread, go for it. Just keep in mind my prior points regarding the effect on your spouse and your older, less savvy self.

For our book exercise, let's assume Dick and Jane want to keep things super-simple. They've taken the Vanguard 2040 retirement target date asset allocation of 77% stocks and 23% fixed income and built it out using 77% VTI (Vanguard Total US Stock Market ETF) and 23% VGIT (Vanguard Intermediate Term US Treasury ETF).

> **Tip:** Notice there are handy contextual help links on the top **and bottom** of the Pralana pages! Make liberal use of them. The content in those pop-up help boxes is excellent, and they won't take you off your page or lose your settings.

Management

Cash Floor and Ceiling

Use the menu to head on over to Build→Financial Assets→Management. The first tab in this section allows you to set a floor and ceiling on your cash account. We haven't really told the tool about our financial accounts yet, so for now assume by "cash account" it means the cumulative value of your checking, savings, and Certificates of Deposits (CDs). You might even include any actual bonds (not bond funds) you hold here. It's important to think about this carefully, as Pralana will use your settings to recommend optimized money moves between your accounts.

For example, if you show that you prefer your cash accounts cumulative total never go below $20,000 (your "floor"), once the calculations hit that bottom it will tell you to withdraw any needed funds from other sources, as part of the guidance and roadmap it lays out. If you tell it the most you're comfortable keeping in your cash accounts (your "ceiling") is $50,000, it will direct you to transfer any perceived overages into your brokerage account for a higher yield.

> NOTE: The tool will project these moves in your withdrawal roadmap when it sees they are mathematically necessary. But be aware, *you* are responsible for making these transactions happen in real life! Of course, the tool isn't tied to your actual accounts and thus is not able or empowered to make these moves for you. It's laying out the steps for you, and those are your financial housekeeping to-do items for a successful financial life. Your doctor may say you need a healthier diet, but you're the one that has to actually implement it.

Most people have some sort of an emergency fund for unexpected car, home, medical type expenses and even job loss. If you're working, one rule of thumb is to have six months of essential, non-discretionary funds in your emergency savings. That's a good rule! Even retirees have emergency funds. Some banks or cash flow/budget tools allow you to create virtual savings buckets for different expenses within your one physical savings account. Our household uses that feature to have virtual funds for annual vacations, holiday gifts/expenses, our next vehicles, and so forth.

You can set different floor and ceiling levels for different time periods. Dick and Jane have a current floor of $10,000 and ceiling of $15,000, but note that it becomes $15,000 and $20,000 when they move into retirement in 2040.

Withdrawal Priority

Move one tab over to Account Withdrawal Priority. This tells the tool where the aforementioned shortage in your cash account will be remedied from. I like a nice, clean roadmap where your planned money moves always keep your immediate spending accounts well topped up, but it's good to establish your preferences here, just in case. Dick and Jane have specified their brokerage account as the first go-to, which is normal as those funds typically have lower tax rates than taking from a pretax IRA, and there could be penalties for tapping a Roth or pretax account before you're eligible.

Later in this book, we'll explore a very cool optimization tool within Pralana that will analyze and set this for you, so don't spend too much time fussing over it. Note that you can change your preferences for different time periods, such as when your Roth funds are fully accessible without penalty. Stick with the tool's defaults when you can, until you get comfortable and learn more.

LTCG Withdrawal Strategy

Let's sashay over another tab to the LTCG Withdrawal Strategy. It stands for Long-Term Capital Gains. I mentioned earlier that if the tool sees that your cash needs would cause your checking/savings to fall below your desired floor amount, it will show a transfer from your taxable brokerage account (or whichever is up next per your Account Withdrawal Priority settings above) to checking/savings.

Here's the rub—if this money is coming from a brokerage account, there are a few ways to tap it. The money in your brokerage account may fall into a few categories. There may be interest, realized gains, tax exempt, and unrealized gains sitting in the account. Realized gains and tax exempt (for example, municipal bond interest) have no tax repercussions when they are withdrawn. Interest is taxed at your regular income tax rate. Unrealized gains are, for example, shares of stocks, stock funds, bond funds, or other assets that have grown in value. That "gain" is called unrealized gains because you haven't sold them yet and "realized" the capital gain. But, if the shares need to be sold to satisfy this withdrawal, they will be realized and part of your tax bill. If you held the shares longer than a year, they're taxed as LTCG. Otherwise, the gain is taxed as regular income. If you've been paid qualified dividends, and haven't reinvested those in new shares, they can be withdrawn as they've been taxed as long-term capital gains when granted.

So, a bit of strategy is in order. If you know you're in a lower income tax bracket than your LTCG bracket, hold off on realizing those gains. If you're in a high income tax bracket, say 24%, you might prefer to grab the assets taxed at 15% LTCG rather than something taxed as income. The setting here conveniently allows you to specify whether you want to withdraw capital gains first, withdraw capital gains last, or just distribute withdrawals evenly from all categories. Of course, when you actually perform the transaction, follow suit so that the planning tool numbers stay in sync with reality.

Most people stick with the default of distributing withdrawals evenly, which is what Dick and Jane have selected. However, if you're in the zero percent long-term capital gains bracket and have a lot of unrealized gains, change this to reflect that preference. This is one of those things that's never going to be pin-point accurate on a year-to-year basis, but will average out pretty closely over time in a long-range planning tool.

Account Fees

Well, here's a wake-up call! Most people don't know what they're paying in fees. The industry loves it. That's the beauty of using an excellent planning tool. All the rocks are lifted, exposing the worms, snakes, and spiders beneath. I discussed in the introduction how expensive it can be to pay someone to manage your investments. If you're doing so, account for that cost here. If you're invested in "managed" funds (meaning, actively managed by fund managers), you're paying those too, so be sure to account for them as well. Find the "expense ratio" of the funds you're invested in. Those are the fees that go to pay the fund managers. If you're in index-based funds, the expense ratios are virtually non-existent, typically around .04%. Me likey!

The point is, do the math and fill in the spaces in this section to account for the fees and expenses associated with your investments. Dick and Jane are paying 0% in their cash (checking/savings), .05% in their taxable (brokerage) account, and .08% in their retirement accounts. That's not bad. It's the benefit of investing in inexpensive index funds, which we'll discuss in more detail later.

Deferred RMDs

When you're working, you're probably socking money away in an employer-sponsored pretax defined contribution retirement plan (for example, 401k, 457b, 403b). Those contributions come off your taxable income while you're working, and sit and grow until you're eligible and start using them. It's common for people to roll their money out of those company retirement accounts and into their own IRA after they leave the company. There are good reasons—the company plan fees are usually higher, there are usually fewer investment choices, and the company can switch custodians any time they want. You may have liked that Fidelity 401k, but one day you log in and find your money's not there—it's at some custodian you never heard of.

When you use the money, you get taxed on the withdrawals as regular income. Uncle Sam starts getting itchy for those tax dollars, and therefore you must take Required Minimum Distributions (RMD) when you get to a certain age (currently either 73 or 75 depending on your birth year). There's a catch, though. As long as you're still working, you aren't forced to take withdrawals from your current company's retirement plan. It's a very nice tax dodge, but why are you still working at that age? It's cool if it's simply what you want to be doing. Or, maybe you didn't make a plan earlier in life, or suffered unexpected misfortune. Either way, this is a bit of a silver lining.

If this is the case for you, simply calculate what percentage of your overall tax-deferred money this employer account comprises, and fill in the percentage on this tab for you and/or your spouse if you have one, and this applies to them. This allows the planning tool to not include these sums in its RMD calculations. Dick and Jane have no deferred RMDs.

Effective Tax Rate

Remember how we just said that the money in your pretax accounts hasn't been taxed yet? That means when you're looking at that balance and smiling, it can be a bit of a buzz kill to realize that money isn't all yours. A chunk of it belongs to good old Uncle Sam. Rappers might call it OPP (Other People's Property), but the IRS calls is IRD (Income in Respect of a Decedent) It's our job to minimize that piece, which is a big reason we're doing all this planning! To figure out how much of it is going to be yours to spend in the future, we've got to figure out how much might belong to the IRS.

The problem here is that the planning tool doesn't want to make the mistake most us of do—total our accounts and property values then subtract our debt and voila, there's our net worth. Not so, we didn't factor in that OPP/IRD. The planning tool is asking you this number so it can factor out that money and give you a more accurate number. If you're going to leave the money to your kids, and want an accurate picture of its spending power after they're done paying taxes on it, then use their anticipated effective tax rate for that period of time. The number you enter here is used for things like optimizing and calculating tax on future Roth conversions, and in the places where the tool allows you the option to see monies in absolute or effective dollars. Absolute dollars don't factor in that tax hit, while effective dollars show spending power after taxes.

So, what do you put here? Lots of folks use 15%, as Dick and Jane have here. If you have a ton of money in your pretax accounts, or other later income, you might use something higher. I highly suggest putting a pin in this, as a later to-do when you finalize your plan. At this stage of the game, most folks who are new to planning don't know their average effective tax rate. However, by the time you're done with your plan, you'll have a much better idea. The tool will show you all those (likely) future effective tax rates! At that point, circle back here and adjust this value if necessary.

Account Growth Settings

The first decision to be made on this tab is whether to use simple or advanced portfolio modeling. With the former choice, you can specify an overall rate of return for each account. For advanced, you specify the expected rate of return for each asset class, then what percentages of those asset classes you have in each account. I prefer advanced, even though I'm usually a simple advocate, because using simple in this case can cause some problems when doing Roth conversion optimizations, and that's a valuable tool we don't want to kneecap. The user manual has some good examples of the distinction.

The planning tool also needs to account for the growth of money in your account. You can tell it to base that on the start of the year and work forward, or use the mid-year growth as a barometer for changes in the account until the year ends. For example, if you have cash/money market or bonds/bond funds, you'll receive interest payments throughout the year. If you have stocks or stock funds, you'll receive dividends throughout the year. As well, those funds or stocks should increase in value over the course of the year. We're going to get into more detail as far as telling the tool how we expect our money to grow, but that's a later step.

For now, you can decide based on account churn. For example, if your accounts are mostly static, not a lot of withdrawals or contributions, start of year is fine. An account with $100,000 on Jan 1 set for 5% account growth (we're talking growth here, not compound interest) will then be projected at $105,000 at the end of the year. Of course, if the tool is recommending or you've indicated there will be withdrawals or contributions, it will subtract those from the balance. We're strictly talking about the growth factor here.

But, if there's going to be a lot of activity in the account throughout the year, for example regular withdrawals and/or contributions, we don't want the tool assuming a flat percentage of growth based on the year's starting balance. If this is the norm in your situation, it's probably better to choose the Mid-Year setting. As of this writing, Mid-Year isn't available yet, so Dick and Jane are set to Start of Year. If the accounts are going to be active throughout the year, I prefer Mid-Year.

That concludes the inputs for Build→Financial Assets→Management. Congratulations!

Account Initial Balances

Head on back to the top Build menu and work your way to Financial Assets→Initial Account Balances. You should find yourself on the first tab, for Taxable Accounts (if not, click it to go there). In this section, you enter your initial account balances for your various accounts. By "initial" we typically mean start-of-year. So, dig out or download those 12/31 statements from the end of last year and use the end of statement balances. Take note of the running total at the top of the page, and make sure it aligns with what you think your financial assets add up to.

TIP: Not all statements end on 12/31, so you may have to look at the transaction listing to find the 12/31 balance. If you simply use a balance as of early January or so, it's not the end of the world. We are planning for the long-term here. To be honest, lots of folks take a shortcut here and just enter their current balance. If you're starting your plan toward the end of the year, it's not such a big deal since you'll be updating this plan each January with new start of year balances. So, don't sweat it if this is a lot of work. Having a plan, even if it's not yet 100% accurate, is better than not having a plan at all.

Taxable Accounts

Taxable accounts are broken into two categories on this page. The first is your cash accounts (checking, savings, CDs, etc.). We discussed those above when we set the floor and ceiling values for them. The second group is the taxable investment accounts, otherwise called brokerage accounts. Start with the cash accounts section, and enter those initial balances (per our discussion in the previous section) for each one. Use the "New" line to add additional accounts as needed. I don't recommend using any sensitive information, such as full account numbers.

Tip: For brevity, you may use two letter combinations for your initials (in case you and spouse/partner have separate accounts) and custodian/bank. For example, I might use "BS TD Checking" for Bob Smith TD Bank checking account, or "JS VG Brokerage" for Janis Smith Vanguard brokerage account.

Our friends Dick and Jane have $3,000 in their checking account and $7,000 in their savings, for $10,000 in cash accounts.

Now fill out the lower section with your taxable investment accounts (brokerage accounts). This can be confusing, since we often see IRA (retirement) accounts referred to as "Traditional IRA Brokerage Account." If it says IRA anywhere in the title, it's an Individual Retirement Account, not the same as a taxable brokerage account. Even the terminology can be confusing! When I was first learning all this, many moons ago, I'd get angry and say, "Well, my traditional pretax IRA *is* taxable!" What the lingo means is taxable, like, today. (Ok, you got me if you're already taking money from your pretax IRA and, of course, it's being taxed.) This may be why the original Excel-based Pralana referred to taxable brokerage accounts as "Regular Accounts." Think of it as a "regular investment account," if you like. For brevity, I'm going to refer to it as a brokerage account.

Dick has a regular brokerage investment account worth $25,000 with $2,000 of unrealized capital gains and $1,000 in capital loss carryover. Jane's is worth $75,000 with $5,000 unrealized capital gains and $1,500 in capital loss carryover. Let's look at those two terms in more detail.

Initial Long-Term Capital Gains Unrealized: When you buy investment shares, if you sell them within a year, your loss or gain over what you originally paid is categorized as a short-term loss or gain, and is taxed like regular income. If you've held them over a year, they are then long-term gains or losses, which are taxed via the long-term capital gains tax brackets. Let's look at an example. You bought 10 shares of Vanguard's VTI fund in 2022 for $200 a share for a total cost of $2,000. In 2024, the share price has risen to $250 a share. The value of your shares has gone up—your investment is now worth $2,500. Since you've held the shares longer than a year, you have a long-term gain of $500, but it's an unrealized gain. *You don't actually realize that $500 gain unless you sell the shares.* Any gain will be reflected in the Federal 1099 form you receive from your brokerage at the end of the year, and you'll have to make it right when you file your annual tax return, if you haven't previously paid the taxes on that win. Pralana needs to know how much unrealized gain is sitting in your brokerage account at the start of the year. You can usually find that number on your statement.

Initial Capital Loss Carryover: In our example above, suppose your shares drop in value to $150 each, and you panic and sell them. You bought for $2,000 and sold for $1,500, so you lost $500. You can write that $500 loss off on your tax return, up to $3,000 per year. Suppose you'd have bought 100 shares instead of ten. You'd then have a $5,000 capital loss, and you can write off $3,000 on your return. The remaining $2,000 would be a capital loss carryover, meaning you can carry it over and claim the remainder on next year's tax return. You can find any remaining capital loss carryover on Schedule D of your last tax return.

Tip: Don't Skip It! A lot of folks just skip these numbers, because they don't know what they mean, or they don't know where to find them. Excluding them impairs Pralana's ability to calculate your taxes. The info is usually there on your taxable brokerage account statements, or when you log in to the website. If in doubt, call your custodian and ask.

Cash Accounts (including checking, savings, money market, CD's etc.)

#	Description	Initial Balance
1	Checking	3,000 ⊗
2	Savings	7,000 ⊗
new		

Taxable Investment Accounts

#	Description	Initial Balance	Initial Long-Term Capital Gains Unrealized	Initial Capital Loss Carryover
1	Dick's Brokerage	25,000	2,000	1,000 ⊗
2	Jane's Brokerage	75,000	5,000	1,500 ⊗

Cash and Taxable Brokerage Accounts

Retirement Accounts

Let's shuffle over one tab to the Retirement Accounts tab. By "retirement accounts," we mean accounts that are intended and/or designed to be used in retirement. This includes regular pretax ("tax deferred") Individual Retirement Accounts (IRAs), 401k, 403b, 457b, SEPP, SIMPLE plans, as well as any Roth-type variants. Let's make a simple distinction. Tax deferred retirement accounts hold your money, it grows (hopefully!) and you don't get taxed on that money until you take it out. In normal cases, that's after age 59 1/2, otherwise you might be penalized (there are exceptions). A big bonus of tax-deferred accounts is that the money you contribute (as well as employer matching) isn't taxed at that time. For example, if you made $100,000 gross and put $20,000 in a pretax retirement account, your taxable income is now $80,000. You get taxed on the other $20,000 when you withdraw it in retirement, hopefully at a lower tax bracket.

The Roth variants of these accounts are different. You don't get that tax break in the year you contribute. You're contributing money you're getting taxed on that year. What's the benefit of those? They grow tax free, and when you take the money out, you don't have to worry about a tax bill, even on the growth! That's a huge bonus. There are some tricky rules and five-year clocks that determine when you're eligible. Those are too complex to go into here. I cover that in *Kiss Your Money Hello*[1], if you need a refresher.

Which should you contribute to? Try to think about it this way—if you're in a low tax bracket currently (perhaps at the start of your career), do the Roth contributions and get that tax-free growth going at a low tax rate. If you're in a high tax bracket currently (maybe in your prime earning years) do the pretax accounts for the tax break now. Wouldn't it be cool if we had a tool to help us with that decision? Wait! We do, and that's why we're here. That's why you're reading this book, and why I wrote it for you.

Ok, back to the scene of the crime. You'll see that this tab asks for the tax-deferred accounts, start-of-year balances, and after-tax contributions for you and your spouse (if you have one) separately. This is because you will probably hit the age for required minimum distributions (RMDs) at different times, and it may be more optimal to convert some of this money to Roth accounts from one or the other of you. In our example, we see Dick has two tax-deferred accounts, $225,000 and $25,000, and Jane has one tax deferred account totaling $50,000. They have no after-tax contributions or Roth accounts. The tool doesn't break Roth accounts out for each spouse, as there are no RMDs to be concerned about.

Build ▶ Financial Assets ▶ Account Initial Balances ⑦ Total: $420,000

| Taxable Accounts | Retirement Accounts | Inherited IRAs | HSA and 529 Accounts |

Tax-Deferred Retirement Accounts (You)

#	Description	Initial Balance	ⓘ After-tax Contributions	
1	Dick's 401k	225,000		⊗
2	Dick's IRA	25,000		⊗
new				

Tax-Deferred Retirement Accounts (Spouse)

#	Description	Initial Balance	ⓘ After-tax Contributions	
1	Jane's 401k	50,000		⊗
new				

Retirement Accounts

TIP: In some cases, you can contribute "after-tax" money to your tax-deferred "pretax" accounts. This means you're putting money in your "pretax" account that you've already paid taxes on! It's very important to track these already-taxed dollars and report them on IRS Form 8606, so you don't get double-taxed when you make withdrawals. It can be messy. Your statements should reflect after-tax money in these accounts—enter the values on this page. If your custodian allows automatic mega-backdoor Roth conversions into a Roth 401k, it's a better tactic. Pralana actually generates a projected 8606 along with your other tax forms, as we'll discuss later.

Inherited IRAs

If you have any inherited IRAs (or expect to receive any in the future), move to the next tab to enter them. Here's where it gets tricky! The rules for taking money from inherited IRAs are ever-changing. If you're unsure of the information you need to enter here, such as the distribution period and RMD start year, contact the custodian that is holding the money. Or read the current IRS rules (if you're going to call them, do so as soon as they open in the morning to avoid long hold times). Be careful. I've seen plenty of cases where someone was sure Auntie Em was leaving them a sweet bundle, only to be surprised when it all goes to Auntie's cat, Whiskers. Try not to be overly presumptuous when doing financial planning. You could always save something like this for an additional scenario, or plug it in later when you might be more certain.

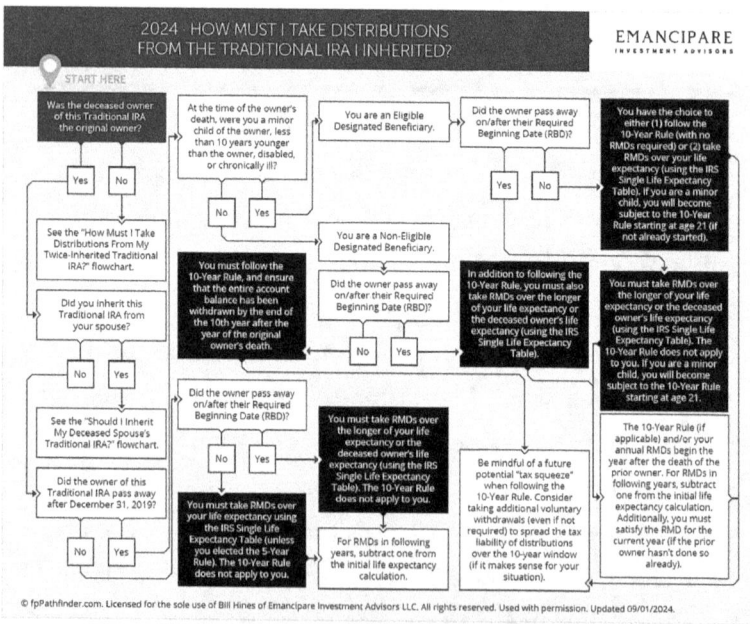

Inherited IRA Distribution Flowchart

This page is like the last one we visited, Retirement Accounts. There are sections to enter an inherited traditional IRA and/or Roth IRA for you and a spouse. If you've already inherited, use the start-of-year balance and the year inherited. You can use a future year and balance (in future dollars) if you believe you will inherit in the future. Pralana only allows you to enter one of each type for you and your spouse, primarily because of the complexity of handing and aggregating these.

NOTE: Prior to January 1, 2020, you could "stretch" the distribution of inherited IRA money over your lifetime. The SECURE Act changed that. Any IRAs inherited on or after that date must now be distributed within ten years. Why? The government has been waiting patiently for its tax revenue! Remember, the money in a tax-deferred IRA isn't all yours. Some of it belongs to the government. As with any pretax account, it is income with respect to a decedent.

The fields here allow you to delay the beginning of distributions to some future year, and then take the money in equal installments over the number of years specified. Required distributions from an inherited IRA usually begin the year after the inheritance occurs, however if the decedent was already making required distributions when they passed away and had not yet done so in the current year, the heir(s) must make that payment.

HSA and 529 Accounts

Still with me? Long chapter here! Move to the last tab in this section, Build→Initial Account Balances→HSA and 529 Accounts.

Now it's time to account for any Health Savings Account (HSA) accounts you may have. These are the golden goose of all accounts, as the money is never taxed! The contributions are pre-tax (like 401k contributions) the earnings grow tax free, and withdrawals aren't taxed as long as you follow the rules. You typically become eligible to open a HSA account if you are on a high-deductible health plan (you knew there had to be a catch!). They are therefore popular with young, healthy people. It's a common strategy to leave the money untouched, perhaps to use for health care expenses in early retirement/FIRE or traditional retirement. Sadly, Dick and Jane have no HSA accounts (yet!).

> TIP: The planning tool doesn't (and shouldn't) assume you are actually going to use this HSA money! It will track your balance and growth, factor in any tax implications, but you have to tell it directly when you plan to withdraw and spend the money. The reason is that due to the triple-tax advantage of HSA accounts, for example, many folks will allow them to grow for a very long time before using them. You can also withdraw it for past eligible expenses, so keep careful track of receipts to document those over the years. If you plan to use HSA money, you need to account for that with scheduled withdrawals, which we'll cover later. 529 spending is accounted for in the section on college expenses.

> NOTE: Pralana doesn't model Health Reimbursement Accounts (HRA) that are sometimes offered by employers. The online help offers helpful advice in handling these—you can reduce your health care premium and out-of-pocket expenses by the amount your employer gives you.

The bottom section asks for year starting balances for any 529 College Savings Accounts. These are funded with after-tax money but grow tax free and aren't taxed when withdrawn and used for qualified education expenses. They have become more popular as the rules for unused college savings have loosened up. You can even roll the unused education funding into a Roth IRA for the beneficiary at some point. 529 plans can even provide a state tax deductions for residents of some states, if you're a resident and invest in your state's plan. You are free to put your money in any state's 529 plan, and some are better than others. So, if you get no explicit benefit from your own state's plan, shop around. Dick and Jane have saved $10,000 for their little munchkins.

Hooray, Dick and Jane have filled in their financial assets (whew!). The good news is that in subsequent updates (you should update your plan every year) you only need to update the start-of-year balances, remove any closed accounts, and add any new ones.

Simple Portfolio Modeling

Do-It-Yourself (DIY) investors are typically comfortable setting up a portfolio of low-cost, diverse index funds. Or, perhaps using a target date fund for the ultimate set it and forget it for retirement or college savings. Financial planning involves a lot more, and can be daunting to the DIY crowd. Too many lose faith in their ability to provide good information, and then fall victim to the financial predators who use financial plans as bait. You can do this!

To do high-fidelity financial planning, you need to make some assumptions. There are huge life decisions under the scope of your lifetime financial roadmap, and I like to be as accurate as possible in order to have the highest level of trust in the results. A lot is banking on this guidance (sorry for the pun)! "Simple" options can be a tempting convenience, but I'm not a fan. Yes, I'm always advocating for simple when possible, but in this case, not at the expense of accuracy, with such big decisions being made.

Rates of Return

That said, let's explore the Build→Financial Assets→Simple Portfolio Modeling page. This page lists the various account types you might have and asks for a real rate of return. It's important to note that on some pages you can specify whether the number you're entering is real or nominal. That isn't the case on this page, you enter real rates of return only.

> TIP: A nominal return is the total rate of return on an investment before deducting taxes, inflation, investment fees, and trading costs. Think of it as the "gross" return, to put it in salary terms. Once you subtract those costs, you have the real return, same as your net pay is your gross pay with all the "stuff" deducted out. In this case, Pralana can't know about all those extraneous costs, so it's simply subtracting your designated inflation (back on Build→Scenario Assumptions→Inflation) from the nominal return to get real return.

This is where you estimate how much your various account types will earn for you. You can leave any you don't have blank. If you plan on using the Advanced Portfolio Modeling, you can ignore this page and skip to that section. The major difference is with this simple option, you put your expected returns and taxation of your taxable brokerage account. With the Advanced option, you will do so by type of investment (stocks, bonds, alternatives, cash, etc.) and then express your asset allocation for each type of account, as well as the taxation on your regular taxable brokerage account.

TIP: Rate of return is often confused with yield. For a savings account, it's simple—they are the same. But for stocks/equities, you earn money both through dividend payments, plus the growth in the share prices over what you paid. Rate of return factors in both, whereas yield on your stocks is solely the dividend and/or interest payments. For example, Vanguard's VTI ETF has a ten-year average return of about 12%, and ten-year average dividend yield of about 1.7% (which is included in the total nominal return of 12%).

So, what should you put in these fields? If you want to be accurate, go through your year-end statements for the last few years and look at the annual summary numbers. Average them out over a ten-year span if possible. I'll give you a few overall average numbers below, but the right numbers for you are highly subjective. For example, checking accounts typically have little to no interest return. Basic savings accounts also have low rates. High-yield savings accounts have much higher interest rates, but may come with strings attached, like minimum balance requirements.

As you can see, for you specifically, this depends on what type of accounts you have, and how much money is in each one. Financial aggregation tools like Quicken Simplifi and Empower can help to get your head around this, but only after they have a few years of history to work with. If you're not sure, you can use my default numbers below, but I recommend you do the homework. Here's an idea of what to use in these fields.

Cash: If all your money is in regular checking/savings with almost no interest return, this would be something on the order of -2% or -3%, after subtracting for 3% average inflation. However, if you're a savvy saver and keep minimal amounts in basic checking/savings, and keep most of your emergency fund and other savings in high yield, you may enter something like 0%. Adjust per your situation, but that's how the thought process would go. Dick and Jane are using 0% as they're savvy savers with high-yield savings accounts.

The rest of the accounts listed here normally contain some investment mix of stocks and fixed income (bonds, cash, real estate, etc.). So, the answer for those completely depends on your asset allocation (how much in stocks vs fixed income/bonds). As we discussed earlier, Dick and Jane are using high-yield savings accounts, and also invested in the Vanguard 2040 target date fund (and not in the fund, but similar in their taxable brokerage account), so if they were using simplified, they'd use 0% for cash. The VFORX fund on Vanguard's page shows around 7.5% rate of return over the last ten years, so they'd use a 4.5% real rate of return in the other accounts.

For other asset allocations, you might just look up a Vanguard target date fund that has a similar allocation, and use those historical returns, or plug your own into an investment tool that will show past returns.

Growth Taxation

This might be the most confusing section you have to enter, and it's likely the one most misinterpreted. Again, this only pertains to only the ***growth*** in your regular, taxable brokerage account. Take note that it's asking what percent of the ***growth*** is attributable to each of the five categories. In this Simple Portfolio Modeling section, it wants that info for the account as a whole, without the individual breakout for different investment types that we'll see for the more advanced portfolio modeling choice.

Simple Interest: Cash, money market, bonds, and bond funds pay interest. Funds that have a mix of stocks and bonds also pay interest. If you or the managers of any active funds you hold sell stock shares that are held less than a year, any gain is taxed as a short-term capital gain, which is at the same rate as interest income.

Qualified Dividends: These are dividends that qualify for the preferred long-term capital gains tax rates. You get taxed on dividend payments even if you choose to reinvest them!

Realized Long-Term Capital Gain: This is common when you're invested in managed funds, where the fund managers are actively trading throughout the year. The fund managers will buy and sell stocks in the fund, and if you have held those shares longer than a year, you will have realized gains in this category.

Long-Term Capital Gain When Withdrawn: This is the "unrealized" gain in the value of your shares over what you paid for them (your basis). You don't get taxed on this until you sell the shares and realize the gain.

Tax-Free: If you hold funds that have tax-free gains, for example municipal bond funds, you'd have some of this.

I recommend you read the related section in the Pralana manual to get this right. You might also look at your 1099 tax forms from your brokerage, and the online information for the funds you're invested in. This is another example of a personal finance task that's much more difficult if your investing portfolio is complex! You may derive the numbers from your brokerage summary reports, or aggregation tools like Empower.

We already said that Dick and Jane have set up their brokerage account as 77% VTI (stocks) and 23% VGIT (bonds). I did a quick check and saw the ten-year average total return (share value gain plus dividends) for VTI is 12.10%. The ten-year average dividend growth is 1.52%. There are no interest, realized gains, or tax-free gains in these two funds. Dividing 1.52 by 12.10 gives 13% of the total growth in the fund over those ten years is qualified dividends, and the other 87% of the growth is in unrealized gain. For VGIT, the ten-year average total return is 10.95% and the dividend (interest) ten-year average is 1.89%. Dividing 1.89 by 10.95 gives 17% of the total growth as interest and 83% as unrealized gain.

Dick and Jane aren't using Simple Portfolio Modeling, but we already said they have an interest in modeling based on the Vanguard VFORX target date fund. If we look at the ten-year average total return for that fund, it's 7.8%. Dividend return is 2.19%. For a more complex managed/active fund like this, you'd have to dig into your statements or the fund documentation to find the nuances of any realized gain during the year because of trading in the fund, or how much if any of that dividend return is actually not LTCG but regular income because of the bonds in the fund. This is another reason people will often choose to replicate funds like this in their portfolios by holding similar allocations and investment choices in simple index funds.

Enough with the simple! Let's move on to the better choice—advanced.

Advanced Portfolio Modeling

Class, please open your (webpage) book to page Build→Financial Assets→Advanced Portfolio Modeling. Let's dig into the details, so we'll have a true high-fidelity financial roadmap.

Portfolio Time Periods

The first tab in this section is Portfolio Time Periods. This allows you to reflect changes you intend to make over the years. For example, you may be a young person with decades until you retire. In that case, your retirement accounts would likely be more aggressively allocated. As you near your goal, you would likely make them more conservative. This feature allows you to tell the tool about those plans. For now, Dick and Jane are going with just the two periods, one starting in the current year labeled Working and one when they move into retirement in 2040.

Asset Class Names

Move over one tab to Asset Class Names. This is simple, in line with our simple theme. You see three asset classes for Dick and Jane—Cash, Stocks, and Bonds. If you're looking at your own config, and have imported it from a previous Pralana Gold (Excel) export file, you may see two residual classes named HSA Assets and 529 Plan Assets. These are explained in the contextual online help for this tab. I'd delete those and keep it simple. You may come from a more complex place in terms of your investing, and possibly have other classes of investments such as alternatives, commodities, and crypto. You would enter those here to properly account for their expected returns on the next tab.

Rates of Return

Let's move over one tab to Rates of Return. For each asset class you defined on the previous page, you'll have to show here what your expected total rate of return is. Unlike the simple mode, you can do this in real (after inflation) or nominal (before inflation) terms.

> TIP: Wherever you get the choice, I recommend using nominal, since using real returns will require you to keep track of the general inflation rate you designated on Build→Scenario Assumptions→Inflation, and each time you change it, you'd have to remember to come here and change these real return numbers as well.

By rate of return, we mean any income or yield thrown off by your investment class, plus any gain (or loss) in the value of the shares. For example, the 150-year average total return of the S&P 500 stock index is a little over 9%. The average historical return for cash (including high-yield savings and money market accounts) is a little over 3%. Corporate bonds typically yield between 4-5% and US Treasury bonds around 3-4%. Dick and Jane have used those numbers to enter an expected nominal rate of return on cash at 3%, bonds at 4%, and stocks of 8% for 2024 to 2040, In 2040, when they plan to become more conservative and move their aggregate bond funds (which hold corporate bonds, among other types) to US Treasury bond funds, they've dialed the expected bond nominal return to 3%. As you can see, they're being conservative by going with the lower end of the historical averages. If the asset classes do better, that's gravy! Keep in mind that by being too conservative, you may also cause your tax liability to be understated.

Growth Taxation

Move over to the Growth Taxation tab. This is essentially the same as we saw in Simple Portfolio Modeling, so see the coverage in the section we just covered, as a guide to these values. In the simple modeling, you're assessing the taxation on the brokerage account. Here, you're breaking it out by your different asset classes, which is much more accurate. You'll also see a small checkbox at the bottom of this page asking if you're reinvesting dividends. See the discussion on dividend strategies in Chapter 2 Money Path Strategies and Tools. If you uncheck this, the tool will assume your dividends are being distributed to your spending (cash) accounts.

Asset Allocation and Location

Move to the final tab on this page, Asset Allocation and Location. On the first sub-tab for this section, Asset Allocation Mode, You have two choices here.

> NOTE: The tabs will change on this page based on which asset allocation mode you choose!

Mode 1: This mode is simpler (yay!). You just go down the list of account types (called asset locations, i.e. taxable brokerage, tax deferred, Roth, etc) and specify your percentage of each asset type (stocks, bonds, cash, anything else you've indicated you have in the earlier step). Enter this information for all the time periods you identified back on the first tab.

Mode 2: This one is a bit more complex. You first specify your desired overall asset allocation (across all accounts as a whole), and then fill out the target asset allocations for each account type just as we did for Mode 1. Using the account priority you specify on the Account Prioritization tab, Pralana will then allocate assets to each account. Once an asset class is fully allocated (per its overall asset allocation), it is no longer available for allocation to subsequent accounts. It's a bit like being in the cafeteria line: those in front get whatever they want until that item is gone and then that items is not available for those still in line.

Mode 2 Example: Assume you have $1,000,000 and an overall allocation of 80% (or $800K) in stocks and 20% (or $200K) in bonds. Assume your Taxable Investment account is the top priority account and has a balance of $500,000 with a target allocation of 60% stocks and 40% bonds. Pralana will allocate it $300K of stocks and $200K of bonds. This fulfills the overall bond allocation of $200K and so no lower priority accounts will be allocated bonds.

But, I digress. Most people have different allocations in their asset locations. If you're a couple, it may well be because you have very different risk tolerance levels, which is a good reason to do things that way. Therefore, I think the simpler Mode 1 is a better choice for most. If you choose Mode 2, the tool will do a bunch of fancy, complex work to move money around (virtually, you should follow suit with the actual recommended transfers) to achieve your desired overall asset allocation. Neither Pralana, nor any other consumer grade planning tool can handle the taxes on this moving around (in taxable brokerage). Dick and Jane are using Mode 1.

Move to the next sub-tab, Asset Location by Account. Because Dick and Jane have modeled their asset allocation after Vanguard's VFORX 2040 target date fund, which is at 77% stocks and 23% bonds, that's how they've set up their accounts in 2024. Below the 2024 asset allocations, we see the new allocations starting in 2040, the year Dick plans to retire. They intend to switch to a more conservative allocation in each of their accounts—10% cash,

30% bonds, 60% stocks. That is effectively a 60/40 asset allocation, which is quite typical for new retirees.

Asset Allocation & Location ⓘ

| Active Asset Allocation Mode | Mode 1: Asset Location by Account |

Mode 1: Specify Asset Location by Account ⓘ

Scenario: 1 ⚫ 2 ○ 3 ○

Define your asset location target % for each account. **The Cash account is not shown as it is always 100% allocated to cash.** See the user manual for more information.

| Copy values from 2024 to other periods |

		Taxable Investment	Your Tax Deferred	Spouse Tax Deferred	Your Inherited IRA	Spouse Inherited IRA	Your Inherited Roth IRA	Spouse Inherited Roth IRA	Roth IRA	HSA	College 529 Plan(s)
2024	Cash	%	%	%	%	%	%	%	%	%	%
	Stocks	77.0 %	77.0 %	77.0 %	77.0 %	77.0 %	77.0 %	77.0 %	77.0 %	77.0 %	77.0 %
	Bonds	23.0 %	23.0 %	23.0 %	23.0 %	23.0 %	23.0 %	23.0 %	23.0 %	23.0 %	23.0 %
Totals: 2024		100.0 %	100.0 %	100.0 %	100.0 %	100.0 %	100.0 %	100.0 %	100.0 %	100.0 %	100.0 %
2040	Cash	10.0 %	10.0 %	10.0 %	10.0 %	10.0 %	10.0 %	10.0 %	10.0 %	10.0 %	10.0 %
	Stocks	60.0 %	60.0 %	60.0 %	60.0 %	60.0 %	60.0 %	60.0 %	60.0 %	60.0 %	60.0 %
	Bonds	30.0 %	30.0 %	30.0 %	30.0 %	30.0 %	30.0 %	30.0 %	30.0 %	30.0 %	30.0 %
Totals: 2040		100.0 %	100.0 %	100.0 %	100.0 %	100.0 %	100.0 %	100.0 %	100.0 %	100.0 %	100.0 %

Asset Location and Allocation

If you're following the bucket strategy, you may tweak this to only hold bucket one (next two years of expenses in cash) cash where the tool is telling you draw it from, and allocating the rest to bonds, as discussed in Chapter 2, Money Path Strategies and Tools.

Some retirees will add additional phases of asset allocation, as you typically no longer need to chase yield as you get into your older years. For ease and simplicity, they've used the same asset allocation in all their accounts. OK, this concludes Advanced Portfolio Modeling, whew.

Scheduled Withdrawals

Dick and Jane are still pre-retirees, so they have entered nothing here, but let's discuss the usage of this feature. Let's take your HSA account (if you have one) for example. Since this is the ultimate tax advantaged account (you never pay taxes on this money), people will keep contributing during their working years, invest it aggressively, and use it in FIRE, early retirement, or traditional retirement health care expenses. Planning tools will not assume you are using the money until you tell them you are planning to use it. That's what you'd use this section of Pralana for. If you've reached a point where you've put those HSA funds to work, and perhaps spend a certain amount per year, enter the values here so the tool can properly track your balance.

Another way to use this section is if you have planned withdrawals, such as following the 4% rule, or some other safe withdrawal strategy, in retirement. Often, spouses or partners will come to some mutual agreement about how much each will contribute to retirement expenses, and this is a good place to reflect that decision.

Lastly, once you feel your plan is complete and locked in, you could take the optimized withdrawal strategy the tool has laid out with the withdrawals for you as ***unscheduled***. You can then plug them in as ***scheduled*** withdrawals here. That will change the reporting from showing unscheduled withdrawals to the more purposefully scheduled withdrawals.

SEPPs

Substantially Equal Periodic Payments (SEPP) are a little-known way to take money out of your pretax retirement accounts prior to the current allowable (without penalty) age of 59 1/2. It's a hack used by the FIRE community, but has some strings attached! If you're interested, read up on Internal Revenue Code Section 72t[2] and implement your strategy on this page of the planning tool. You

---

2. https://www.irs.gov/retirement-plans/substantially-equal-p eriodic-payments

can enter one for yourself, and one for your spouse, if you have one.

Personal Loans

This section is not for personal loans you have taken out! You may have made loans to others, usually family members. This page is where you can reflect that expected (ha!) income in terms of installments and any interest there might be for current loans or ones you intend to make in the future. Dick and Jane have not gone down this road, so there are no entries here.

Investment Loans

This is where you'd reflect any loans you have that aren't related to personal property. If you have a loan on your home (mortgage), vehicles, toys, or other property, it's best placed in the Personal Property section of the tool. Enter the details for other loans, such as personal loans, credit cards you don't pay off each month, and margin loans on investments. Dick and Jane are debt-averse, so they have no entries in this section.

You've finished entering the details of your financial assets, hooray! Don't forget, revisit this section each January to enter your start-of-year numbers.

CHAPTER FIVE

INPUT YOUR INCOME

JOBS, SIDE HUSTLES, PENSIONS, SOCIAL SECURITY, OH MY!

WE'VE TOLD THE PLANNING tool all about your basic info, assumptions, and financial assets. This chapter will focus on your income—now and in the future. Move to the Build→Income→Employment page to get started. If you've shown you're a couple, you'll see radio buttons at the top of the page to select each person. The screen is identical for each of you.

Employment Income

Let's start by having a look at Dick's current employment income. We see his job listed as "Dick's Current Gig"—whimsical and I love it. I'm not a fan of putting on too much personal detail when it's unnecessary. You could use acronyms or abbreviations or even pet names for your employer (keep it clean, now!). He started this job at age 40. You can enter a specific date, a year, an age, or 'R' in this field (to indicate the day of your retirement specified in Build→Get Started→Scenario Assumptions). Yes, you may indeed intend to begin a fun part-time or full-time gig in retirement! It's not so much about not working as it is about living every day on your own terms. I've seen plenty of highly paid professionals "retire" and become garden experts at home improvement stores or Uber drivers. You have to do something with your time, and might as well think about making it tax deductible (this allows write-offs for things like mileage, cell phones, internet, car washes, and so forth). That said, if you started the job prior to this year, it doesn't matter what you put, so you don't need to go doing a bunch of research on that if you aren't sure. Just put last year.

The same goes for your employment stop date. Using 'R' means you don't have to keep changing it here if you change your intended retirement date back on the getting started screen. Be aware that if you put an age value, Pralana will use your birthday to determine when that income starts or stops. We see that Dick's current salary is $125,000, with an expected 3% (nominal) average raise per year. He's putting away $12,500 in pretax per year (probably a 401k) with an employer 50% match of $6,250 (also pretax). You'll see there are plenty of fields on this page to show annual contributions to Roth, HSA, and defined benefit plans, as well as after-tax contributions to pretax accounts (we discussed those and the related pitfalls in the last chapter).

There are some checkboxes at the bottom of the page. These are related to self-employment or 1099 type jobs. If you're running a LLC or sole proprietorship, or just doing simple non-W2 gigs like side hustles as a driver, delivery person, or other. For those types of jobs, you normally get paid as a contractor, not an employee. That means there are no Social Security and other typical W-2 paycheck deductions. In that case, you'd check the box to disable SS contributions.

The next box asks if this is a self-employment job. If you're running your own business, there are lots of complexities that a personal planning software tool won't model, such as your business expenses, deductions, taxes, and so forth. If you check this box, you then put your *net* (after expenses) income in the top Annual Gross Income field. The field is a bit misnamed in this case, but we have to roll with it. The last checkbox asks if your business is eligible for the QBI deduction provided by the Tax Cuts and Jobs Act of 2017 (which is currently slated to expire at the end of 2025). You can refer to your last return to see if this was employed. Keep in mind, if Congress doesn't extend the legislation, this break will go away.

There is an additional set of vertical columns that allow more employment income streams (current or future) to be described. Dick has none planned. If we have a look at Jane, we see she's making $40,000 per year with a 3% nominal increase, and plans to stop at her earlier specified retirement date. She's contributing ten percent of her income ($4,000) to a pretax account with no employer match.

Employment Income ⓘ

Enter information about your employment income sources.

Person: Dick ◉   Jane ○

	#1
Description	Dick's Current Gig
ⓘ Start	40
ⓘ Stop	R
ⓘ $ Annual Gross Income	125,000
ⓘ Annual Increase	3.0 %
ⓘ Annual % Increase Real or Nominal?	Nominal ⌄
ⓘ $ Personal Contribution to Tax-Deferred Accounts (Pre-Tax)	12,500
ⓘ $ Personal Contribution to Tax-Deferred Accounts (After-Tax)	
$ Company Matching on Tax-Deferred Accounts	6,250

Dick's Income

Employment Income ⓘ

Enter information about your employment income sources.

Person: Dick ○   Jane ◉

	#1
Description	Jane's Current Gig
ⓘ Start	38
ⓘ Stop	R
ⓘ $ Annual Gross Income	40,000
ⓘ Annual Increase	3.0 %
ⓘ Annual % Increase Real or Nominal?	Nominal ⌄
ⓘ $ Personal Contribution to Tax-Deferred Accounts (Pre-Tax)	4,000

Jane's Income

> TIP: If you make annual contributions to pretax and/or Roth accounts when you file your taxes (or before), add those to whatever you're contributing out of your paycheck on this page so they're accounted for.

Pension

A what? While the days of workers starting and finishing their careers with the same employer, and being rewarded with a nice pension upon retirement are gone, some lucky folks still receive them. Dick has indicated he'll be collecting a $100,000 per year private pension at age 65, with a 50% survivor benefit. Note that these values should be entered in future dollars and there is a calculator on the page to help you make that conversion. If you're super lucky and your pension has an annual increase to keep up with inflation, you can enter that here as a real or nominal percentage.

You can show that a certain percentage is non-taxable (perhaps your basis paid in after-tax), and you can reflect that you're going to surrender or roll over some or all of the pension to a Roth or traditional IRA. Switching over to Jane, we see she's got a $50,000 per year private pension coming at age 65.

Social Security

Well, here's a big one! While pensions are primarily a thing of the past, at least most of us still have Social Security coming. It may seem simple, but there are many nuances and opportunities to optimize your benefit (and also lots of poor advice and misinformation!). The people at the Social Security Administration (SSA) are overworked, underpaid, and undertrained. Double check anything they tell you, and try to get it in writing. There are many Social Security calculators out there, some free and some cost money. None of them will take the entire context of your financial world into account like Pralana's built-in tool.

To prepare to address this topic, the best thing you can do is log in or create your account at ssa.gov, and download your latest statement if you aren't already collecting. Two key things on that statement are your full retirement age (FRA) which is when the

SSA will award your "full" benefit, and your Primary Insurance Amount (PIA) which is the amount you will be paid at your FRA. The planning tool will need to know the PIA. Keep in mind that if you're still working, these amounts will change. Put this on your list of things to update when you do your annual housekeeping each January!

TIP: Most of the advice you see is to wait as long as possible to collect. The SSA wouldn't feel too bad if you died before collecting, of course! Your benefit grows the longer you wait. It grows by an annual cost of living increase (if inflation has been up) and your 'reward' for waiting. You get the COLA part whether you wait or collect. When you collect, you get any annual cost-of-living increase the SSA decides to dole out. When I game out the difference between waiting or collecting early with clients, there usually isn't a big difference overall, unless they're folks that will rely primarily on Social Security in retirement. Often, people will choose to collect earlier if they have poor health, or feel they can do better by investing the money themselves. Or, you may decide to wait as it's a nice inflation-protected insurance policy against inflation and late life long-term care costs. Use the optimizer on this page, then the Sensitivities tool or your additional scenarios to see what difference it makes for *you*. There's also a great tool at the SSA page [1] that doesn't require any login. Just select your birth year.

---

1. https://www.ssa.gov/benefits/retirement/planner/agereduction.html

Move to Build→Income→Social Security and make sure you're on the Inputs tab. The planning tool has used your birthdays to calculate your FRA, and that is noted at the top of the page. Both Dick and Jane reach their FRA at age 67. This is another reason to always use your correct birthday (some people might be tempted to use a slightly different date for privacy or vanity reasons). They have both entered that they expect to collect their benefit at age 67. We'll revisit that choice later, when we do some optimization. Dick's current expected PIA at FRA (note I keep using those acronyms to burn them into your brain) is $30,000 per year and Jane's is $22,000. Make sure you don't put the monthly amount! If one spouse's benefit is half or less of the other's benefit, you may be candidates to do a spousal benefit strategy. Pralana will consider this when optimizing, or will calculate it if your inputs show it's at play. But, as always, it's your job to actually file the paperwork with the SSA. As well, this can change over time if you're still working. By the time you're retired, it may not be a thing or the math may no longer support it.

> TIP: There are some good SS tools out there, besides the main SS site I mentioned in the tip above. Two are opensocial security.com (free) and maximizemysocialsecurity.com (paid). Keep in mind they operate in a vacuum—they don't optimize based on the full scope of your financial picture and goals as Pralana's does.

If you've ever worked at a job that doesn't take part in the Social Security program (they weren't taking your half of the contributions from your paycheck and they weren't making the employer half of the contributions) your benefits will be affected. This adjustment is called the Windfall Elimination Program (WEP) when it affects you. It's called the Government Pension Offset (GPO) when it affects your spouse's survivor benefit, should you pass away. If you fall into this category, check with your former employer and the SSA to ensure you're planning on the proper level of benefit. The planning tool has fields on this page to enter those adjustments. You'd make the correction directly in the field for your own benefit, and enter any impact on your spouse in the field provided.

For those skeptical about the SSA's ability to continue COLA increases and wanting to model it, you can make that change here. You can also account for any decrease in benefits you might experience. For example, if you're collecting prior to your FRA and exceed the earned income amounts you're allowed from a job, they will dock your benefit (don't worry, you get the money back with higher payments after you turn FRA). You'll get a notice about the reduction, and can enter the change on this page.

If you're already receiving benefits, just enter your current annual benefit amount (before any taxes you may have them taking out). When you're done entering your information, you can go to the top of the page and click on the Benefit Projections tab to see your calculated yearly payments.

Windfalls

Ah, wouldn't it be nice if that email from the Nigerian Prince claiming to be holding all that money for you turned out to be legit? If it were, you could enter it on this page (Build→Income→Windfall). There are other, more likely reasons you may have a future windfall coming to you. Perhaps it's some kind of stock or other reward from an employer that you'll become vested in. Maybe a family member or other person has told you they're planning on leaving something behind for you. Note that inherited IRAs go in the Build→Financial Assets→Initial Balances→Inherited IRAs section. Indicate the proper taxation. Inheritances and life insurance payouts typically aren't taxable, but lottery winnings, stock options and other windfalls from employers are. Use future dollars, and there's a handy calculator on the page to do that math.

Dick has entered a $5,000 non-taxable windfall for 2025, and a $125,000 taxable windfall for 2030. Jane has entered a $7,500 non-taxable windfall for 2032, and a $10,000 taxable one for 2035.

> TIP: It can be tempting to count on that promised money and enter it here. But many of the windfall categories are those that might not come to fruition. With stock options (below), your employer may go belly up, or change ownership and cancel promised benefits, or even let you go. That friend or relative may forget to name you in their insurance or will, or change their mind and never tell you. These blue sky scenarios may be better reserved for an optimistic scenario. You don't want to bank your retirement success on something that may not occur. If it happens, it's gravy, and go take a nice vacation or buy that boat or RV you've had your eye on!

Another common type of windfall is stock options. These are wonderful incentives from employers, but can have complex rules. In a nutshell, an employer will give you the right to buy shares of company stock at a set price, sometime in the future (when you become 'vested'). The idea is that the stock option grant is at today's prices, and when you become eligible to buy them, they're worth much more, hence it's a good bargain. If you're granted the right to buy at $100/share, and two years later when you're vested, the going price is $150/share, it's a steal. However, you have to use your own cash to buy the shares, unless your employer allows for a cashless purchase (they'll give you just the gain if you decide to exercise and immediately sell enough shares to cover the basis cost). This can be problematic in a planning tool. Yes, the gain is a 'windfall,' but how do you know what the stock will be worth years into the future? You'll have to do some guesstimating. Maybe look at the average share price increase (or loss!) over the past five years and use that. Pay attention to today's dollars versus future dollars, as well.

There are different types of stock options. For example, Incentive Stock Options (ISOs) and Non-Qualified Stock Options (NSOs). There are variants like Restricted Stock Units (RSUs) and Restricted Stock Awards (RSAs). You'll have to dig into the details of yours to determine the details, especially the taxation. Use that information to enter your windfall. One great thing about the organizational process of financial planning is that it motivates you to learn up on the nuances of your personal finances. This knowledge kills uncertainty and is quite beneficial to you and your family. Make sure to take notes so you don't forget those details! Be very careful as these offers can expire over time, and in a short window if you decide to leave the company or they decide to leave you.

Annuities

You can enter your annuities at Build→Income→Annuities. Read that long contract carefully and pester your agent for any details you aren't sure of. It's not a fun process, but it will be enlightening and you'll learn a lot about what you bought and how it works. It allows you to be accurate in your planning, especially in this complex area. Dick and Jane have bought no annuities, so they have no entries here.

Other Income

Head to Build→Income→Other Income. This is a catch-all area for anything that may not have fit well into the other categories. Think child support, alimony, distributions from trusts, things like that. It's flexible in that you can start and stop periods, different types of taxation, and annual increases. Dick has entered $5,000 of annual other income from age 44 to age 49, taxed as regular income. Jane has $6,000 from age 40 until her passing, taxed as regular income.

CHAPTER SIX

EXTRAPOLATE YOUR EXPENSES

PHASE IN YOUR DREAM FINANCIAL LIFE

HEY, YOU STILL WITH me? We've come so far! C'mon now, you can do this. All we need to do is enter your expenses, and we can get some actual, for real results! Think about how exciting that will be, because this part is kind of yucky. Nobody wants to come to terms with their spending, that monster in the closet. The good news is it's not as hard as you might think. And if it's a problem, there's a whole book called *Kiss Your Money Hello (and Financial Stress Goodbye)*[1] by yours truly that will show you how to fix the old problemo. No more monsters!

It's considered a pain to track expenses or to budget. It doesn't have to be that hard! There are some pretty wonderful tools that will do most of the work if you simply plug them into your spending accounts, which should comprise a checking account

---

1. https://books2read.com/kissyourmoneyhello

and perhaps one credit card (keep it simple!). Tools like Simplifi[2] and Monarch Money[3] will do a pretty good job of tracking your spending, cash flow, even investments. They can categorize most transactions automatically, leaving only a little touch-up for trips to generic stores like Costco, where you may buy stuff in different categories. If you try tools like this, go with the basic functions at first, before going down any more complex features. You can also get a good idea by looking at your annual summary for credit card statements, pay stub deductions, checking/savings from the past year.

Personal Property

We've already covered your financial assets. Now let's tell the tool about your personal property. These items, particularly the high-dollar ones (homes, vehicles, toys...) also have an ebb and flow throughout your financial life. They may grow in value, will probably decrease in value, and will be replaced over time. We should account for that, as these transactions are often expensive and need to be factored in.

Property Info

Let's get started. Head to Build→Expenses→Personal Property, and the first tab on that page, Property Info. Dick and Jane have done a good job of laying out their expected property ownership,

---

2. https://app.simplifimoney.com/

3. https://www.monarchmoney.com/

purchases, and sales! Financial planning isn't just about, "When can I retire?" That's why I don't like to call it retirement planning! It's truly a roadmap, a money path for the rest of your financial life—the theme of this book. Let's discuss each item.

They have a primary home (residence) they purchased in 2015 for $175,000 (your original purchase price is your cost basis). They estimate its current worth at $240,000. The real appreciation rate is left blank, which means zero percent, which means they expect the home to appreciate at the rate of inflation, which is about correct historically for real estate. They plan to sell it in 2042 and have factored in 6% for closing costs. Closing costs will involve a variety of expenses such as realtor commissions, taxes, admin fees, and inspections. Bear in mind that due to a recent settlement, the old 6% realtor commission is gone—be sure to research what your commission might be as a buyer or seller and factor it in to any home sale or purchase. You might even factor in your moving costs here. If not, put them under miscellaneous expenses (which we'll cover soon).

TIP: Be careful about bias in estimating your home's current value. Don't go by what a neighbor sold for. Claim the home at zillow.com and update the details. Zillow will then put its powerful comparative engines to work to give you a good estimate. I have an entire book, *Show and Sell 2023* [4], that will save you tons of money when buying or selling homes.

Checking one line further down in the personal property list, we see what Dick and Jane have planned. This line shows they intend

---

4. https://books2read.com/showandsell2023

to purchase their next primary home in 2042, just as Jill is retiring, and pay $300,000. There is no selling date indicated, so it appears they intend to leave this home behind when they pass. Note that for future purchases, you don't enter a "currently own" cost basis. You put the expected purchase price in the Current Market Value field.

> TIP: Don't be confused by that Sales Closing Costs column. It's only for when you sell a property, not when you buy! Of course, you pay closing costs in either case. When you're buying, you'll have to estimate what your closing costs might be and enter them on the Build→Expenses→Miscellaneous page.

On line three, we see they intend to purchase a sailboat in 2025 for $75,000 and enjoy it until 2050, then sell it. They believe it will depreciate at a 5% real rate which after 3% inflation is factored in means 2% nominal depreciation. When buying fun stuff, remember to include any auxiliary expenses (boat dock fees, RV storage fees...) in your expense planning.

Next we see the roadmap for their cars. They have a car bought in 2020 for $40,000 with a current market value of $30,000 and a real depreciation rate of 10%. They plan to sell it in 2030. Their other car is listed below that, purchased in 2017 for $40,000 with a current market value of $25,000 and they plan to sell this one at the ten-year mark, in 2027. Cars three and four follow that, each to be purchased when the current vehicle is sold (in 2027 and 2030) for $40,000. Clearly, they have a strategy of purchasing cars for $40,000 and holding them for ten years! Finally, car number five is listed, to be purchased in 2040, and at that point as Dick will be retiring, they plan to get by with just one car going forward. We'll see about that!

Property Info ⓘ

Enter information about your property

Seq	Property Description	Asset Type	Year of Acquisition	Cost Basis for Assets You Currently Own	Current Market Value	Real Appreciation Rate	Year You Expect to Sell	Sales Closing Costs	
#1	Current home	Primary home ˅	2015	175,000	240,000	%	2042	6.0 %	⊗
#2	Retirement home	Primary home ˅	2042		300,000	%	yyyy	%	⊗
#3	Sailboat	Other ˅	2025		75,000	-5.0 %	2050	%	⊗
#4	Car1	Other ˅	2020	40,000	30,000	-10.0 %	2030	%	⊗
#5	Car2	Other ˅	2017	40,000	25,000	-10.0 %	2027	%	⊗
#6	Car3	Other ˅	2027		40,000	-10.0 %	2037	%	⊗
#7	Car4	Other ˅	2030		40,000	-10.0 %	2040	%	⊗
#8	Car5	Other ˅	2040		40,000	-10.0 %	yyyy	%	⊗

Property Info

> TIP: Be very careful about the Real *Appreciation* Rate in this section for property. It is real, so inflation is factored in. Dick and Jane have left the home blank, meaning it will appreciate at our specified rate of inflation (3%). By using -5% for the sailboat, they are expecting it to depreciate 2% per year (3% inflation minus 5%). They expect the cars to depreciate at 7% a year. You can check the math by heading to the income tabular projections, where you'll see Car1 being sold in 2030, as specified here. Income from sale of property says $19,410 (future dollars), which is today's $30,000 value depreciated by 7% per year for six years.

Existing Loans

Shuffle over one tab to Existing Loans and the first sub-tab, First Lien. This is where you'll describe any original loans for the properties you listed on the previous tab. It looks like they've done a great job on their mortgage—only $13,227 left to pay off as of the start of the plan year on Jan 1. Their principal and interest is $1,134.65 per month and their interest rate is 5.375%.

> TIP: This is another common mistake! I often see clients plug in their actual mortgage payment, which usually includes things like principal, interest, escrow, property taxes. To properly amortize your loan, the planning tool requires the amount of your payment that is only principal and interest combined from the start of the year (January payment)

Dick and Jane have a loan on their newest car. There's a $29,363 balance and $662.99 monthly payment at 4% interest. Pay that buggy off too, kids! There are tabs for home equity loans and home equity lines of credit. They're pretty simple, and Dick and Jane have none, so we'll bypass those areas.

A very cool feature is the Loan Amortization tab. This is a good way to check your numbers. Select each loan you have and ensure it's being paid off when you think it is. For example, a thirty-year mortgage should be paid off in thirty years. If you don't see that, something is off in the numbers you've provided, so revisit those until it looks correct. We see Dick and Jane's mortgage is in the list (to be paid off this year!), their sailboat loan (future purchase, we'll cover that next), and the car loan.

Existing Loans ⑦

Enter information about existing loans (as of the start of this plan) on your properties.

First Lien | Home Equity Loan | Home Equity Line of Credit | Loan Amortization

For real estate, enter information about your current first mortgage. For other types of property, enter information about your the current (first lien) loan.

#	Property	① Balance at Plan Start	① Monthly Payment	② Interest Rate	① Early Payoff Year	① Excess Annual Payment Amount	① Excess Annual Payment Start Year	① Excess Annual Payment Stop Year	① Notes	
1	Current home ⌄	13,227	1,134.65	5.375 %	yyyy		yyyy	yyyy		⊗
2	Car2 ⌄	29,363	662.99	4.000 %	yyyy		yyyy	yyyy		⊗

Existing Loans

New Loans

The next tab in this series is New Loans. This is where Dick and Jane have specified they intend to take out a five-year $56,250 (today's dollars) loan at 5% to pay for that sailboat. If we scroll through the Refinance, Home Equity, Home Equity Line of Credit tabs, we see they have no plans to do that, but if you do, enter the values in those areas.

Operating Cost Categories

Move to the upper group of tabs on this page and select Operating Cost Categories. It's important to tie property-related expenses to the property. For example, a big family house will have different insurance, heating, cooling, taxes, and other costs than the cabin you may downsize to after becoming empty nesters. The big 'ol pickup truck will have a different energy profile than a Prius Prime you may switch up to.

> TIP: If you're renting, you could put your monthly rent and utility expenses in the Phased Expenses with other random expenses. But, I recommend putting it here in the property info instead, as that gives you additional flexibility to change all the related expenses if you buy a home. Remember, each property has its own expense profile, even renting. You simply mark the rental as "sold" in the year you buy your home, if you do that.

This section is empty for out-of-the box Pralana. Here are the categories I like to use as a starting point—Maintenance, HOA,

Electric, Gas/Propane/Oil, Water, Sewer, Rent (if renting, we'll explain later), Trash/Recycling, and Gasoline. Dick and Jane don't have HOA or Rent and have combined Water, Sewer and Trash into one category (they probably pay one provider for all these services.

Operating Costs

Move to the Operating Costs tab, where we can put those categories to work. The properties defined earlier are listed vertically down the page and the cost categories are shown horizontally across the top. This forms a grid to enter annual expenses. Be careful, as many of us budget monthly, it's easy to put monthly values in the fields! The first few columns have predefined categories for Property Taxes, any tax adjustments your state may make for those over 65 years old, and insurance related to the property. There's a column for the total annual operating costs that is updated as you enter numbers.

Following those, you see the columns for the cost categories you have defined in the last tab. For their current home, Dick and Jane have entered $4,000 in annual property taxes, $1,500 in homeowner's insurance, $1,200 for maintenance, $1,800 for electricity, $900 for gas heat, and $1,800 for water/sewer/trash. For their future retirement home, the numbers are $5,000 property taxes, $2,000 insurance, $1,200 for maintenance, $1,800 for electricity, $500 gas heat and $1,000 water/sewer/trash. The future sailboat will cost $1,000 for insurance and $750 for maintenance. All their current and future cars have $500 for insurance, $1,200 for gasoline, and $1,200 for maintenance.

Improvements

The next tab allows you to list capital improvements for your home. This is important, especially for non-primary residence homes, as itemizing the capital improvements can help you with any future tax bill (they are added to your cost basis). They increase the value of your property. Capital improvements are big-ticket items such as additions and decks. They don't include normal maintenance like driveway repaving. Dick and Jane have none of these planned.

Reverse Mortgages

There's a tab for Reverse Mortgages. These used to be very scammy products when they first came out, but legislation changed that to protect consumers. They are still expensive, complex products with very aggressive salespeople (and washed-up actors on advertisements!). They would allow cash-strapped seniors to pull the equity from a home they don't wish to sell, but with lots of strings attached, and likely headaches for their heirs to sort through. Also, the lender can swing on by at any time and assess whether the home is "well maintained" enough. If it's not up to their standards, they can foreclose. This is more likely to occur as homeowners age. If this happens, they're now looking for a place to live. Dick and Jane have no reverse mortgages.

Cash Flow

The last tab in this section is informative and awesome. The Cash Flow and Cash Flow by Property tabs give you very nice summary information. This is great for spot-checking your numbers, so don't just fly by it. There's a lot of dense info, so think about taking advantage of the ability to just download and print a PDF and mark it up by the pool with a glass of vino.

Rental Property

Dick and Jane have no rental property, but let's talk about this section a little, as it's not uncommon for folks to have rental/investment properties. This is an important section if you do, so do some digging. You get no pass on profit (long-term gain) when you sell these, so it's important to have your ducks in a row. You need to know things like your depreciation period and improvement percentage (how much of the property value is the structure versus the land). Last, you enter your annual rental income for the property and by what percentage you typically raise it. The rest of the tabs on this page are like the primary home tabs, except for the last one, where you show if the property is eligible for a QBI deduction per the Tax Cuts and Jobs Act of 2017.

Children

Ah, the rug rats! Past, present, future. I have a wonderful young couple as clients, and we added "Baby TBD" to their plan to ensure 'lil TBD's expenses are accounted for right up to and through college. TBD is allegedly on their own after that (we'll see...). Everyone says your home is your biggest financial decision. Nah, it's kids, and a bigger decision in ways other than money! Not everyone wants to be parents, but if you do, it's important to account for the future expense. Let's get going on that. First, head to Build→Get Started→My Family and make sure your kids are listed at the bottom of the page! Dick and Jane have two kids—John born in 2008 and Sue born in 2010.

Pre-College Expense Categories

Head to Build→Expenses→Children and make sure the first tab, Pre-College Expense Categories, is selected. This is great, because it allows you to factor in kids' costs for the time they're with you, and those expenses automatically drop off after they've flown the coop, leaving you with an empty nest. I joked, but it's not uncommon for kids to hang around even after graduating high school, college, tech, or trade school or in any case while they're trying to get their feet under them. I'm all for it! As long as they're treated like the adults they are, and taking some responsibility, pulling their weight by paying their own phones, car insurance, and other costs. Adulting!

The categories I typically use here are Food & Drink, Clothing, Health Insurance, Cell Phone, Entertainment, Education. That last one is for education expenses up through high school. It could include supplies, costs of school trips, and tuition if they're attending private school. Dick and Jane agree, as these are the categories they're using.

Pre-College Expenses

Move over one tab to Pre-College Expenses. The pre-college expense categories are on this tab. John and Sue's annual expenses are $3,000 food & drink, $1,500 clothing, $500 health insurance, $600 cell phone, $1,200 entertainment, and $1,200 education, for $8,000 each. This plan is being built while the kids are well along, approximately ages sixteen and fourteen, so expenses should be fairly close to actual as they are real and can be measured. For future kids, you might do a little research and find the average annual cost of raising kids up through high school graduation. I've seen numbers at around $20,000.

Pre-College Expenses ⑦

Scenario: 1 ◉   2 ○   3 ○

Description	John	Sue
Food & drink	3,000	3,000
Clothing	1,500	1,500
Health Insurance	500	500
Cell phone	600	600
Entertainment	1,200	1,200
Primary education (thru HS)	1,200	1,200
	8,000	8,000

Pre-College Expenses

College Expenses

When you've completed that section, move one tab to College Expenses. This tab can apply to any higher education, such as trade or tech schools. These expenses can be scary! There's an entire chapter on hacks to save money in this category in *Kiss Your Money Hello*[5] . The good thing about creating your lifetime financial roadmap is that it forces you to sort through all these big decisions. I've seen clients get to this section, and consider that they haven't even talked to their kids about it yet. If they're old enough to think

---

5. https://books2read.com/kissyourmoneyhello

about it, their input is valuable. Lots of kids are taking a pass at expensive colleges and going to faster and less pricey alternatives like community colleges, trade or tech schools, online learning, military enlistment, or going right into the workforce.

> TIP: If they want to do that "gap year," ask what they plan to do with their time and how they plan to pay for their expenses! I know it's not my business, but I've seen too many cases where doting parents sacrifice the years they should enjoy by spending too much on adult children.

Getting back to filling out the page, there are tons of resources to game these expenses out. For each child, enter the year they will start, the annual expenses in today's dollars (all expenses, including books, room, board, etc.), how many years they expect to go, and what percent of the costs you plan on spending. It might be less than all of it because the kids may pay a portion, or relatives, or you expect grants and scholarships. There's a drop-down list asking how you intend to pay, with the choices being Pay as you go, 529 Plan, and Student Loans. This should only be loans you will pay, not ones that are the responsibility of the kids. If you choose this option, also enter an interest rate and term. The columns to the right will calculate some useful numbers. There is also a useful tab to show you the amortization of the loans. Spot check that to ensure it looks correct.

Dick and Jane have shown they expect John to start in 2026, go for four years at a cost of $25,000 per year (pretty low by today's standards, so likely in-state college and perhaps commuting!), and they'll be paying 75% of that (perhaps expecting grants, scholarships, or help from family) using their 529 plan money. Sue will start in 2028 with the same duration and expense, but they expect to use a student loan for her at 5% for eight years. You can view the amortization schedule for that loan on the final tab, Student Loan Amortization. Make sure it ends when you expect it to, or something is wrong.

College Expenses ⓘ

Scenario: 1 ⦿ 2 ○ 3 ○

	ⓘ College Start Year	ⓘ Annual College Costs in Today's $	ⓘ # of Years in College	ⓘ % of the Cost You Plan to Fund	ⓘ How Do You Intend to Fund Each Education?	Loan term (years)	ⓘ Actual or Assumed Interest Rate	ⓘ Your Share of the Cost in Future $	ⓘ Your Total 529 Plan Contributions	ⓘ Total Estimated Cost of College
John	2026	25,000	4	75 %	529 Plan ⌄		%	86,118	64,346	64,346
Sue	2028	25,000	4	75 %	Student Loan ⌄	8	5.000 %	93,145	0	115,292
					Total cost in future dollars:			179,263	64,346	179,638

College Expenses

> TIP: Please be careful about going into debt to pay for your kids' education. Perhaps talk to your children about having **them** take the loans out, if needed. It's an investment in their future, after all. It teaches adulting and as they have a big stake in the game, it could motivate them to do their very best. If you're taking a parent loan with the agreement that they'll take over payments after they graduate and get their first job, make sure it's in writing. I've seen cases of short-term memory loss in otherwise healthy youngsters disrupt the family dynamic when it comes time to pay the piper! You've likely worked hard and gotten them this far. Don't forget to focus on the rest of **your** life!

Healthcare

Here's another very important section that takes a bit of work and research to do correctly. This will probably be your biggest expense in retirement, so spend some time on it. This is another 'phased' section, with the phases laid out based on the inputs you've provided for your birthdate and retirement dates. There may be phases showing as both of you working, one of you working, neither working, one on Medicare, and both on Medicare. You can show that you're using the Affordable Care Act (ACA) for any of the phases, but it's usually deployed when someone is no longer working and not yet eligible for Medicare.

If you're still working a full-time job, your health insurance is likely through your employer benefits, with some amount of it paid by the company and some by you. Typically, your part of the premium is taken out of your paycheck pretax, just like your 401k contributions. Your plan probably has an out-of-pocket maximum. Some people might put their out-of-pocket max in the out-of-pocket expenses field, but you should really shoot for accuracy by tracking your annual expenses for copays, deductibles, coinsurances, and other medical expenses, and use that number. Not doing so could mess up your tax projections!

Enter your annual premiums here, and if they're all taken out pretax, put 100% in the box for percent of pretax premiums. Likewise, if you're running a small business and paying for health care through that as a business deduction, enter the percent in that box instead.

Affordable Care Act (ACA)

Let's talk about the ACA, as this is the trickiest part and also where I see a lot of mistakes made. The healthcare.gov website is your friend. It will ask you to put in your zip code, and if it determines your state has its own ACA portal, it will direct you there. The sites have facilities to sign up for coverage, and also some sort of quickie calculator or plan cost estimator tool that doesn't require you to provide all the details you would in signing up. You give it the basic, anonymous info, and it shows you the plan costs.

If your income is low enough, you will receive a Premium Tax Credit (subsidy). Even if your income is high, your costs are capped at a percentage of your income. The costs vary around the country, so it's important to give your correct zip code. You'll want to get a list of plans and costs after entering your family info and who you need coverage for. Filter those results to show only silver plans, and then sort them from least expensive to most expensive. Make sure you're looking at the unsubsidized cost and pick the second lowest cost one. So, not the cheapest one at the top, but the one just below it. Take that annual premium cost total for your family (not just you) and enter it in the field in the planning tool for ACA second lowest cost silver plan premium.

You need to do this even if you aren't picking that plan, because it's used as a benchmark in calculating your subsidy. Now select the plan your most likely to use, total that annual premium for your family, and put it in the Insurance premiums field. Based on the plan benefits and your typical spending (you may have to project this for future years) put in an out-of-pocket spending number. Tick the box that asks if ACA should be assumed if available, for any time periods you intend to use it. With this information, the planning tool will calculate any subsidies you should receive and factor them into your spending for each year.

TIP: Be careful with taxable events like big Roth conversions, or they could push your income higher and result in you having to pay back those ACA subsidies! They could also make your Medicare premiums higher, if you're on Medicare.

Medicare

This part is simple, and it's hard! You can check the box at the top to allow the planning tool to calculate the base Medicare premiums for original (or, standard) Medicare part B (regular care) and D (prescriptions). Part A is for hospitalization, and there are no premiums for that. The tool will take care of annual premium increases. There's a thing called Income Related Monthly Adjustment Amount (IRMAA) that will cause your premiums to be higher if you pass certain income levels (which are pretty high, so not a concern for most folks). There is a two-year look-back period, since the agency must have some way to check your income. They'll look at your tax filings for the past two years to determine if you should pay an IRMAA surcharge. That's why you see the fields at the top to enter your Medicare Modified Adjusted Gross Income (MAGI), so the tool can also do the math. This can all be tricky, and this isn't a book about Medicare. The tool will calculate your MAGI as well, and try to keep you from IRMAA when you're doing certain optimizations. If Medicare is over two years away, don't worry about those two fields for MAGI. We'll talk more about IRMAA later, so put a thumbtack on that thought.

Based on what I just said, you might recognize a problem. What if you just retired at age 65, and have no income (other than perhaps Social Security, pension, etc.). You can imagine Medicare doing their two-year look-back, back to those years you were working, and assessing an IRMAA surcharge based on that. It's exactly what will happen if your income from those years exceeds the limits! Not fair, right? You fix it by filing a form SSA-44 to show you've had a "life-changing event," in this case, retirement, and no longer have that income. They'll remove the IRMAA. Do it as soon as you file to start Medicare. In the meantime, you can reflect this in Pralana by reducing those MAGI entries for the prior two years. This will remove the IRMAA penalties that the tool is calculating (see those at Review→Tabular Projections→Expenses→Specified Expense Details→Healthcare).

Standard Medicare doesn't cover dental care, eye care, podiatry, and a few other things. Most people supplement standard Medicare with either a Medigap or Advantage plan to add coverage for those other items. You should do some serious research before choosing one of these plans! The commercials can be very deceptive and the "experts" that say they'll guide you are working on commission, and an unethical one will push the plan on you that works the best for their wallet. You'll pay extra for those additional plans, so you'll have to factor that in when you enter values in the fields for your premiums and out-of-pocket costs. Be careful not to add in the base Medicare part, though! What you enter here is the extra for the Medigap or Advantage.

Wrapping up Healthcare

All that said, let's see what Dick and Jane are up to. Their first period is the current one, where they're both working. They're spending $2,500 on annual premiums and $500 in out-of-pocket expenses. The premiums are 100% tax deductible, as they're likely coming out of one or both of their paychecks. The numbers are identical for period 2, when one of them is working. Dick has retired by now, so it's likely they're getting their insurance from Jane's employment benefits. If you check the helpful dates, that period only lasts four and a half months, as Dick then hits age 65 and goes on Medicare. Don't risk going without insurance, even for that small gap in time! Murphy is always lurking, so don't risk a medical event that can throw your retirement plan into chaos.

Period three is when both are retired, and one (Dick) is on Medicare. Now you see the box checked to assume Affordable Care Act insurance for Jane. This period is from 2041 to 2043, and we know that back on Build→Getting Started→Scenario Assumptions they plan to have moved from California to Texas by this time. Let's assume Plano, TX zip code 75023 and check the healthcare.gov site. Using the quick calculator shows that the second lowest silver cost plan is $427/month, or $5,124 per year. So we enter that in the field for the second lowest silver cost plan. Jane wants a plan with some premium features, like dental, so she goes with a more expensive silver plan that costs $7,104 a year. Dick has chosen a Medicare Advantage plan that costs $2,400 a year. Adding those, we get total annual healthcare premiums of $10,104. They've entered that number and put the breakout in the notes field for their own reference. They've calculated a $3,000 out-of-pocket cost based on their coverages and current health status. Later, we'll likely see most of that ACA premium removed because of the Premium Tax Credit subsidies.

Period four is when they're both on Medicare. Jane is also using an Advantage plan at $2,400 a year, so that added to Dick's gives them a $4,800 annual premium. They've kept the $3,000 out-of-pocket expense. The last bit of business on this page is to put the amount these expenses will decrease upon the passing of the first of them. They're indicating 40%, which is fairly normal and conservative as opposed to thinking costs will simply just divide in half. Often, the passing of a spouse causes a fast degeneration in the health of the remaining one.

Healthcare Expenses ⓘ

Scenario: 1 ⦿ 2 ○ 3 ○

Period	Start Date	End Date	Insurance premiums	Out-of-pocket expenses	% Insurance premiums paid with pre-tax $	% Out-of-pocket expenses paid with pre-tax $	% Considered business deduction	Assume ACA insurance if eligible?	ACA second lowest cost silver plan premium	Notes
Period 1: Both working	01/02/24	12/31/39	2,500	500	100 %	%	%	○		
Period 2: One working	01/01/40	05/15/41	2,500	500	100 %	%	%	○		
Period 4: Retired, one on Medicare	05/16/41	07/13/43	10,104	3,000	%	%	%	☑	5,124	$7104 ACA, $2400 MCA
Period 5: Both on Medicare	07/14/43	07/13/68	4,800	3,000	%	%	%			

Healthcare Costs

Long Term Care Expenses

Well, here's another thing that's hard to think about, but must be planned for! The good news, like everything else in our mission here, is when it's all done you can sleep well at night. No more awkward conversations or thoughts between family members. Your spouse may be worried about this, your kids might be worried you'll become a burden on them at the worst time, when they're already dealing with young kids. Grab yourself some peace of mind!

> TIP: If you have long-term care insurance, I'd put those premiums under phased or miscellaneous expenses, not here. This is for the actual costs of care out of your pocket when the time comes. The planning tool figures in the tax-deductibility of these expenses. The insurance premiums aren't always deductible, for example, when they are in a rider on another type of insurance, such as an annuity.

Will you ever need it? Who knows! Check your family lineage for hints. Our moms are 88 and 94 and living on their own. The men in my family tend to keel over suddenly from heart attacks while otherwise robust mentally and physically. I'm not a fan of LTC insurance as I've seen too many cases where it's not there (at least not how you think) when clients have needed it. They often have long delay periods, i.e. their financial help doesn't kick in until you've been paying on your own for some period of months. I've seen folks pass away during that period, thus having paid it all themselves, with no help from the insurance company after years of paying high premiums. They're less likely to cover the things that really will keep you incapacitated for a long time—dementia, Alzheimer's, Parkinson's. Policies can be sold off to less viable insurers, perhaps off-shore. Insurance companies sometimes go broke and out of business. State bailout programs aren't guaranteed.

If it's not obvious by now, I'm a big fan of self-funding. Build that cost in. If you never need it, that's a good thing. You can leave it behind to your spouse, family, or a needy charity. The big question then becomes, what kind would you prefer, and how much should you have put aside? There are lots of options these days, from in-home care, to assisted living communities, to full nursing home care. If you need it and don't have the money, you'll still be taken care of under Medicaid but your options will be limited. You may be asked to sell any property you still hold to help pay, depending on circumstances like whether a spouse still needs to live there.

I point my clients to the Genworth calculator[6] as one of our exercises together. It's run by an insurance company, so take the results with a grain of salt as they're probably over-inflated to move you toward buying the insurance. It's a good tool, though. I recommend setting it to providing an annual cost, current year, and plug in the zip code you think you might want to be, and check the

---

6. https://www.genworth.com/aging-and-you/finances/cost-of-care

results. You'll see estimates for the various categories. I said to use the current year because you put the amounts into the planning tool in today's dollars, and it will apply the LTC inflation rate you specified earlier on Build→Get Started→Scenario Assumptions.

Dick hasn't specified any long-term care costs for himself, but Jane has entered $36,000 per year starting at age 86 until she passes.

Term Life Insurance

This page allows either spouse to enter information about their term life policies. It's pretty straightforward, asking for only the policy start year, policy term, death benefit (future dollars), and total annual premium (today's dollars). Keep in mind that the planning tool won't show this income unless you're setting the life expectancy age such that the policy comes into force. Make sure you don't double count this income by also putting it in Build→Income→Windfall.

> NOTE: The older Pralana Gold (Excel) version has a term life insurance calculator tool in it, to help you determine if term life insurance is needed, for whom, and how much. It's not yet implemented in Pralana Online as of this writing. To be honest, I hadn't used it much. When I feel a client plan is done, one exercise is to simulate each person passing away prematurely. If those exercises show plan failure, that's a good sign some term life insurance is necessary.

Dick and Jane have no term life insurance, so let's move on.

Cash Value Life Insurance

As you can probably guess, if you've been reading, I'm not a fan. This insurance product falls into the realm of complex, expensive, and risky. As I mentioned back in the discussion on annuities, they can be sold to off-shore companies that don't follow our strict rules in the USA. Insurance companies can go bankrupt, and the state bailout funds aren't guaranteed. The sales pitches used for these products, such as Indexed Universal Life (IUL) are typically quite deceptive.

They don't call it "whole life" for nothin'! Most clients I've worked with have no need for life insurance after their kids are done with college. Why continue paying all that money until the day you die? You're far better off investing it yourself, with no middle-persons to pay or hope they give you a cut of the earnings on the money you turned over to them.

That said, if you own it, you own it. As with annuities, read the contracts carefully and make sure you understand every nuance in the fine print. Use the knowledge to fill out this page. The other downside of owning complex products with lots of gimmicks, "features," riders, and so forth is that it can be very hard to emulate them using planning tools, as they can't account for every variability. A nice feature here is that the second tab does a nice job of projecting your benefits. Dick and Jane have no cash value life insurance.

Charity

I'm often apprehensive when I get to this section with clients. I get sad when I see they're not doing any charitable giving, but I understand why. They come in worried they're not going to retire at all, so they're holding back in this area. After we've worked it all out and their plan shows they're in far better shape than they had thought, I say a secret prayer that they'll pad this section out a bit.

There are great tax benefits to charitable giving, and it can be fun. If you have a particular year that's going to have a big tax hit because of selling an investment property or some other good fortune, you can mitigate it by creating a donor advised fund (DAF) and bunching your giving in to one year. It's hard these days to get a tax break on charitable giving, unless you do enough to surpass the standard deduction and can itemize (this may be possible for other reasons already, such as high medical costs). Then you have a nice fund to invest and dole out for years, deciding who will get the benefit of your philanthropy. You can spend it down, then refund it in high-tax years for another tax break, rinse and repeat as necessary.

> NOTE: Donor advised funds/charitable trusts are not yet implemented in Pralana Online as of this writing, but they are in Pralana Gold (Excel).

This page has fields for the description of the beneficiary of your giving, the annual amount, start year and end year (if any). Easy peasy so far. You can check the COLA box if you increase your giving each year based on inflation. The next two fields are related to Qualified Charitable Distributions (QCD). You have to be at least age 70 1/2 to do these. The benefit is that they are made out of your pre-tax IRA account, thus helping to decrease your Required Minimum Distributions and therefore, your taxation.

> TIP: You have to actually have crossed over 70 years, six months to do QCDs. It's not one of those "in the year you turn 70 1/2" deals.

If you indicate you'll be doing QCD, the tool will continue assuming the charitable giving comes out of your cash accounts, until it sees you've passed 70 1/2, and then it will assume the money is coming out of the IRA. You can show on each line if that one is for your IRA or your spouse.

Dick and Jane have no charitable giving thus far. I'll discuss the benefits in our planning meeting :-)

Phased Expenses

Here's another fun exercise. I guess some folks would consider having to gather all this information, thinking about all this morbid stuff, a kind of financial drudgery. If that's how it's beginning to feel, think of it this way—you're painting the masterpiece of the rest of your life. When it's done, you're going to be so happy to stand back and behold what is possible! The beautiful rest-of-your-life that awaits you. Keep going, we're almost there!

Take this exercise, for example. We're going to assess the "rest" of your expenses, now that we've covered healthcare, property, kids' education, insurances, and taxes. Now we get to the good stuff, and you get to tell the tool how much fun you're going to have over the rest of your life.

Time Periods

Start on Build→Expenses→Phased Expenses. The first tab asks you to lay out some time periods. Some ideas are both working, one working, both retired (early retirement go-go years when you're hitting that bucket list hard), the slow-go years when you hit your 70s and may no longer be rock climbing and kayaking, and finally the no-go years in your 80s when you become more sedentary, probably eat less, travel little. Figure out what years represent those timeframes for you and enter them here, along with some notes. Dick and Jane are going with 2024 (current), 2040 (retiring), and 2050 (getting older). You can have up to five, a big improvement over the three in Pralana Gold/Excel! Keep in mind you don't need one for when the kids finish school, if you entered their expense detail in Build→Expenses→Children→Pre-College Expenses.

Categories

Slide over to the next tab, where you'll enter expense categories. Here's a list I usually start with.

Essential: Groceries, Dining Out, Toiletries, Personal Care, Pet, Internet, Phones.

Non-Essential: Clothing, Cleaning/Laundry (DIY if things get tough), Gifts, Vacation, Pocket Money/ATM, Subscriptions, Gym/Training, Entertainment/Hobbies.

> TIP: You might question some of these. Dining out is essential? The problem here is that in a dire circumstance, where you're cutting non-essential spending, you'd need more for groceries if you're no longer dining out. So, I leave it there as a conservative pad. Most people have plenty of clothes, and don't need to buy more if they're cutting back on spending. Also, if you have things that will be tax deductible, put them in the next tab (Miscellaneous) as there's a way to account for the tax break there.

% Reduction for Survivor

The next tab asks what percentage do you want to reduce these expenses by if one of you passes away. I recommend 40%, as some will stay the same (internet, for example). If you're a Gucci/Prada aficionado and your spouse is more into Great Value, adjust as necessary.

Amounts

Next hit the Amounts tab. This is where we lay it all out. I'd put in your current expenses first, filling out that first column. Then evaluate each expense for the later phases in terms of how you think you might spend at that age. Don't short yourself, be realistic. I see too many folks so tired of going to work, they're desperate to retire and take shortcuts here to try to will the math into working. Keep in mind you have to do something with your time—have a plan for that and what it might cost. You don't want to be that person sitting around the tavern all day complaining about the weather.

Remember that you've covered your kids in many of these categories already, so factor their expense out. Let's check out what Dick and Jane are up to.

Period 1 (2024): Groceries $8,400, Dining Out $2,400, Clothes $1,200, Gifts $1,500, Hobbies and Entertainment $2,500, Vacation $6,000, Household Items $2,400, Pocket Money/ATM $2,400, Pet $1,200, Subscriptions $1,200, Internet $1,000, Cell Phones $2,400.

Period 2 (2040, both entering retirement): Groceries $12,000, Dining out $10,000, Clothes $600, Gifts $1,500, Hobbies and Entertainment $5,000, Vacation $12,000, Household Items $2,400, Pocket Money/ATM $3,600, Pet $1,200, Subscriptions $1,200, Internet $1,000, Cell Phones $2,400.

Period 3 (2050, both into 70s): Groceries $6,000, Dining out $5,000, Clothes $300, Gifts $1,500, Hobbies and Entertainment $2,500, Vacation $10,000, Household Items $2,000, Pocket Money/ATM $2,400, Pet $0 (Aw!), Subscriptions $1,000, Internet $1,000, Cell Phones $2,400.

I think I'd add another period for when they get into their 80s. Those expenses will likely be less (except for healthcare, which is accounted for elsewhere) so this is conservative, and they can add it during a later update. The last tab shows the projected totals by year, including essential and non-essential breakouts. Pay close attention here, ensure this spending is realistic and in line with your plans, as it's critical to an accurate plan success. As I mentioned in the beginning of this chapter, you'd do well to use a good low-touch app to monitor your spending and cash flow, at least at a high level.

Phased Expense Amounts ⓘ

Scenario: 1 ◉   2 ○   3 ○

Enter the amount of essential expenses (in today's $) by category and time period below.
The amounts will be adjusted for inflation using your general inflation rate(s).
Use the other tabs to edit the time periods and expense categories.

#	Description	ⓘ Essential Expense?	Period starting 2024	Period starting 2040	Period starting 2050
1	Groceries	✓	8,400	8,400	6,000
2	Dining Out	✓	2,400	10,000	5,000
3	Clothes		1,500	600	300
4	Gifts		1,500	1,500	1,500
5	Hobbies and entertainment		2,500	5,000	2,500
6	Vacation		6,000	12,000	10,000
7	Household Items	✓	2,400	2,400	2,000
8	Pocket Money/ATM		2,400	3,600	2,400
9	Pet		1,200	1,200	
10	Subscriptions		1,200	1,200	1,200
11	Internet	✓	1,000	1,000	1,000
12	Cell Phones	✓	2,400	2,400	2,400
	Total Essential:		16,600	24,200	16,400
	Total Nonessential:		16,300	25,100	17,900

Phased Expenses

Miscellaneous

Use this section for any expenses that are one-time or limited du-
ration (in years), and/or have tax deductions associated with them
(alimony, child support, etc). Think about things like whether you
intend to help your kids with their weddings, or a down payment
on their first home. That kind of thing goes here! But not those
related to property or health care, put those in the areas we already
covered for those expenses. You can show if there's an annual
cost-of-living update and whether the expense is essential. We see

nothing listed here, so I guess little John and Sue are on their own, and should start saving for their weddings and first homes!

OMG, we're done entering expenses! Whew. All done, take a break, go spend some of that dining out budget. The hard part is over now. Let's get ready to have some fun.

Chapter Seven

Review and Reporting

Measure Twice, Cut Once.

Tabular Projections	Graphical Projections	Reports
Income	Savings & Net Worth	Report Setup
Expenses	Sources of Income	Plan Inputs Report
Cash Flow	Tax Projections	Plan Results Report
Balance Sheet	Asset Allocation	Tax Forms
Portfolio	Key Metrics by Scenario	
Account Statements		
Scenario Assumptions		

Review Menu

EVEN THOUGH THE HARD part is done, we don't want to rush off and run our first analysis just yet. I don't want you to be overly bummed or overly exuberant if the data isn't correct! A good way to do a spot-check is to take a spin through the summary report pages. We've already seen a few places where the planning tool shows you this kind of info in context, such as the loan amortization tab for property loans.

NOTE: We're covering review and reporting now because it's important as a spot-check after entering your data, before you go much further. However, you also want to come back here after you're done with all the other pieces of creating your roadmap—when all the tweaking and tuning are done. Then you'll get the full benefit of this information and what it's telling you.

Tabular Projections

Head to Review→Tabular Projections→Income and the first tab (Income Statement). This page is cool beans, because it shows your income from various sources for the rest of your life. You can see the work income, Social Security (when it kicks in), pensions, windfalls, sale of property, and other income. Scroll through and make sure it all makes sense to you! If you're more of a paper person, note that each of these areas has a Create PDF button to download as a PDF to print out. Spreadsheet nerds can export to that format as well.

It might help to set to today's dollars first. When we do that, we see Dick and Jane's employment income at $165,000 per year until Dick retires, then two years at $40,000, which is Jane's employment income until she retires. Now set that to future dollars. See how the numbers change to reflect that 3% per year increase we set earlier in the tool? Notice that some number are underlined (hyperlinked). Social Security is a good example. If you move down the list to when Dick has passed, and click on Jane's Social Security benefit, a "Metric MRI" (Pralana-speak!) pop-up will appear that shows where that money is coming from—her death benefit has occurred. This is a powerful feature to get into the details when something doesn't look right, and great for troubleshooting. Note that the pop-up numbers are in future dollars! Explore the other tabs here—Income Details and Payroll Contributions (which you may cross-check against your pay stub). Get down in the weeds to ensure everything is correct. Your retirement success depends on it!

Next, head to Review→Tabular Projections→Expenses and do the same type of review. Buried in here, on that third tab (Taxes), is an absolute goldmine of tax information. Don't forget to scroll right, as it won't all fit on one page! You'll see your projected effective and marginal rates by year, with cap space remaining in that marginal bracket (great for topping it off with a Roth conversion if you'd like). This is another critical area to check against your actual return when it's done. If they're not in the ballpark, something is wrong in the planning data (or...perhaps your CPA didn't have all the info they needed).

Review→Tabular Projections→Cash Flow, Cash Flow Statement tab is another very useful page. This one shows the ebb and flow of your financial life. It's easy to see where the tool thinks your cash accounts (checking/savings) will overflow your preferred ceiling and want you to move that amount to your brokerage for better returns. Another good end-of-year check—did that actually happen? If not, why? If you fell short, perhaps there were unexpected expenses, or you weren't accurate in your expense projections. Move to the Withdrawals tab on this page. The tool is showing you where you should take your spending money from each year. You can simply take this information and set up monthly withdrawals for the next year (dividing the number by 12) and put things on autopilot. It's just like getting a paycheck during the working years. The last tab shows any planned annuity purchases.

Pull up Review→Tabular Projections→Balance sheet. This will be the go-to report for many folks, and actually a good place to start your review. It shows your asset location balances, liabilities, and net worth year-by-year and almost all the fields on this page are hyperlinked to drill into the detail behind the numbers.

TIP: In these pages, it's a good troubleshooting technique to click the Show Empty Columns and see what might be missing. For example, seeing an empty pension column in the income projections is a reminder you forgot about that old pension you're vested in.

Next, head to Review→Tabular Projections→Portfolio. Scan down the Rates of Return tab to ensure these projections are in line with those you typically get and expect going forward in the various account classes. Same with the Growth tab. Don't forget the today's dollars vs future dollars button at the top! This one allows you to see how each account should grow over time, pretty nifty. The Allocations tab is much more involved than you'd expect. There's a wealth of information here that, again, should correlate with reality. The final tab is a year-by-year list of Roth conversions, as well as the limiting factor. We haven't discussed that optimization yet, so put a pin in it for now. This is one you might print and stick on the fridge or put in your calendar for an end-of-year reminder, as they have to be done by December 31 (don't wait until the last week, or they may not process in time).

Next up is Review→Tabular Projections→Account Statements. This is an outgrowth from the old summary report in Pralana Gold/Excel. That one (cough, a result of a suggestion by yours truly) gave a five-year roadmap type of view of to-do list items such as moving cash ceiling overflows to the brokerage, withdrawals from various accounts to pay expenses, Roth conversions, and more. A high-precision planning tool like Pralana will lay out the roadmap for the rest of your life, which is likely decades. We know some of that far out stuff is pretty fuzzy, as there will always be new legislation and so forth to change things up (see: Secure Act I, Secure Act II...). The next five years, though, should be pretty solid. People can focus on and digest that, so that's the reason I asked the Pralana team to build that summary report. It was a lot of work doing it manually for each client. This version of it in Pralana Online goes much further, giving you that basic account-level summary for the rest of your years. Want the five-year summary version? Just don't scroll over that far, or export it to PDF or spreadsheet using the handy buttons on this page, and print or cut as necessary. I use this one all the time to build five-year to-do lists for clients, and you should too!

> TIP: Always pay attention to the projected movement of money in these screens! Remember, the planning tool isn't connected to your accounts. It cannot move the money for you. It is assuming you are behaving in line with what it's projecting, because you have told it this is what your habit is. For example, "When our checking savings (cash ceiling) gets above $50,000, we usually move it to our brokerage and invest it for higher returns..."). Maybe the AI version will someday do that for us, who knows.

The final tabular projection is at Review-Tabular Projections→Scenario Assumptions. It's a condensed view of your assumptions around inflation, state of residence, tax filing status, and cash floor/ceiling. A nice touch here is that it can show the cumulative effect of the inflation at the start of the year and end of the year (in case you aren't already having trouble sleeping...).

Graphical Projections

Let's move to the middle column under the Review menu, Graphical Projections. Some of us are visual learners, after all! These are wonderful snapshots of data. Pull up the first graph, Savings and Net Worth. The graph allows you to see your asset categories in proportion to one another, including your property. I use it to show clients that might get scarily low on financial assets that they still have an excellent lever to pull—massive equity in their property. It provides immediate relief and stimulates discussions whether they might want to sell, capture that equity, downsize to something maintenance free, and enjoy the rest of their lives stress-free. Of course, reverse mortgages are another way, if they really don't want to sell the property, but I'm not a fan of those. Often they're thinking of leaving the childhood home to the kids, who, secretly, aren't really interested and don't want to deal with the hassle of emptying a lifetime of clutter and the stress and complexity of selling a home as a group. I've seen it tear folks apart.

> TIP: Of course, if there's a huge long-term capital gain tax bill related to this, you'd have to think twice. If the kids inherit the primary residence, they inherit at the cost basis, and the capital gain tax disappears.

This graph also shows the ebb and flow of income and expenses over the rest of your life, represented by solid lines. Make sure that looks correct. You should see spikes when property is bought and sold, or long-term care expenses kick in, windfalls occur, and so forth. Dig in and make sure they represent reality and not an extra zero fat-fingered during data entry. You can hover over the graph to get excellent numeric detail! Dick and Jane notice a big spike in the middle of the graph—big income and expense in 2042. What's going on there? Hold that thought, we'll find out in a sec!

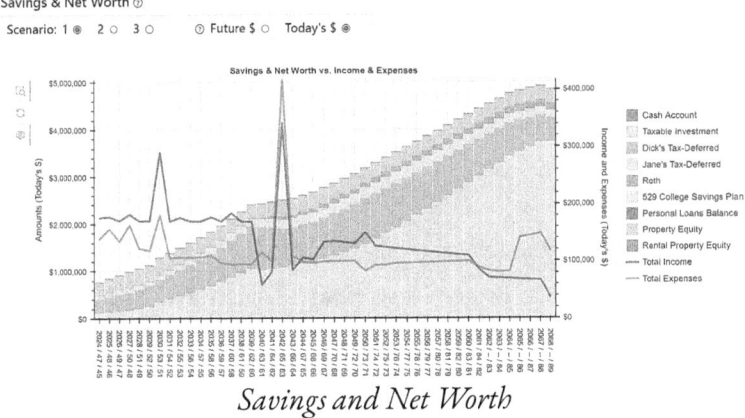

Savings and Net Worth

Pull up the next graph at Review→Graphical Projections→Sources of Income. Wowza, that's what we were just wondering about! Sure enough, you see the big bar in the middle as income from the sale of a property. Oh, right, they're planning to sell that year. We covered it when entering all their property info. They're also buying the retirement house. Big income, big expense. It all checks out. This graph is a good way to see where your money is coming from over the years. You'll see it transitioning from employment income to other sources, such as pensions, annuities, Social Security, sale of property, and windfalls. You can hover over the bars to get more precise numeric detail on any year.

Sources of Income ⓘ

Scenario: 1 ⦿   2 ○   3 ○   ⓘ Future $ ○   Today's $ ⦿

This chart shows spendable income from external sources as well as cash from household assets. The sum of these is the **Total Cash Inflows** on the Cash Flow Statement.*
*Note: to maintain compatibility with PRC Excel, the Total Spendable Income metric on the Income and Cash Flow Statements does not deduct payroll taxes.
The spendable Employment income shown in this chart does exclude payroll taxes.

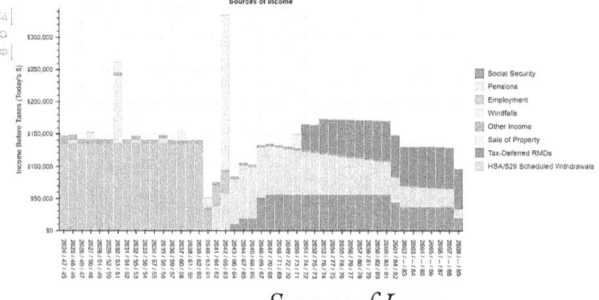

Sources of Income

Let's look at some tax graphs. Move down to the next graph at Review→Graphical Projections→Tax Projections. There are two graphs on this page. Tax trends are illustrated by the top graph, and that's important. For example, you might see the typical tax barbell, where you're paying high taxes while working (especially in those pre-retirement peak earning years), then see a series of low-tax years in early retirement (perhaps while living off savings and not yet starting Social Security and IRA distributions), then a trend of high taxes later, when you're forced to take required minimum distributions (RMDs) from your pretax IRAs. Who wants to be paying high taxes in retirement? Nobody, ever. A graph flow like that makes it really easy to see that you might want to balance it out by doing Roth conversions during those low-tax rate years, to balance things out and keep you in a lower tax bracket when you need to take those RMDs, avoiding the retiree tax bomb. The working years will even show your payroll contributions to Social Security and Medicare taxes.

The lower graph shows details on some key tax metrics, such as adjusted gross income, deductions, and capital gains or losses. It can be a good way to monitor things like AGI if you're receiving

Affordable Health Care subsidies. Again, you can hover on either of these graphs for numeric details.

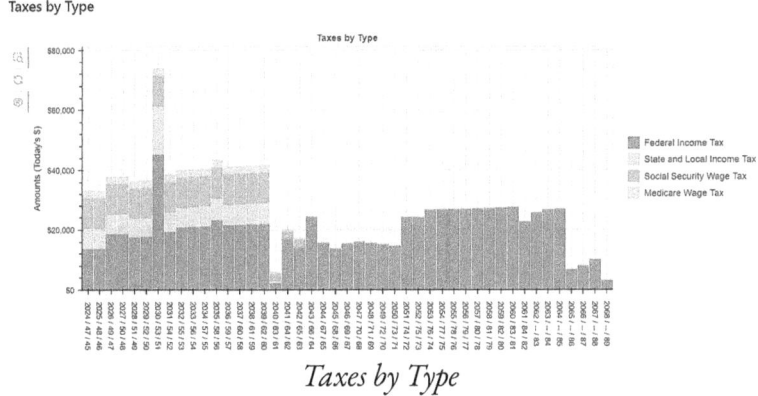

Taxes by Type

There's an asset allocation map at Review→Graphical Projections→Asset Allocation that shows the projected growth of your financial assets over time (not counting property). It's useful to ensure your allocation is staying in line with your risk tolerance, income needs, and time horizon. Look for any erratic changes in the graph and find out why they're occurring. Perhaps when you first set up the tool, you didn't have any inherited accounts, and didn't pay attention to the asset allocation setting for those, and it was way off. Then you inherited something, added the amount, but didn't adjust the allocation setting. You should keep your asset allocation in line with those each year as part of end-of-year financial housekeeping.

Finally, Review→Graphical Projections→Key Metrics by Scenario is a powerful view of the deltas between your various scenarios. We're still walking through an initial, baseline scenario here (which you should always establish first!). We'll talk about adding additional scenarios later, and how this graph is a great way to spot-check the difference between them and how each one affects your financial life. It's a great bird's-eye view of how the different scenarios affect your savings, net worth, and expenses over the rest of your life.

Reports

We spend so much time in front of a computer screen doing this work, it can be exhausting and stressful on our eyes and minds. That's a recipe for mistakes! For that reason, I recommend printing off the inputs report and looking it over with a handy marker and highlighter to ensure the numbers look correct. It should also be downloaded as another form of backup in case you overwrite something valuable, or you lose your plan data.

The output report also provides a concise way to look over what the tool is telling you, and excellent fodder to post up on your fridge or desk to remind and motivate. If you don't have a color printer, bring (or email) the PDF to an office supply store and they'll create nice multicolor copies for a few bucks.

> NOTE: Review→Reports→Tax Forms will produce sample approximate projections for your 1040, worksheets, and related forms for the current and future years. What?! This wasn't in the old Excel versions, and it a fantastic addition! I love the ability to take these and compare them to the actual returns in order to sanity check the plan inputs, as well as to do some preliminary tax planning toward the end of the year. However, the US tax code is complex. Pralana is not a tax preparation tool, only a guide.

That concludes our coverage of the Review major task area. One more to go! Now we get to the fun stuff, running analysis, optimizing, building scenarios, and maintaining your plan.

## CHAPTER EIGHT

LET'S ANALYZE AND GET SOME ANSWERS!

AND THE WINNER IS...YOU!

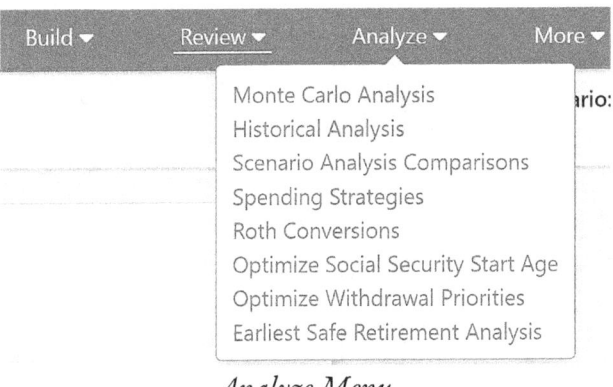

Analyze Menu

Monte Carlo Analysis

WE'VE DONE OUR PART (or, Dick and Jane have!), so let's now harness the true power of the planning tool to get some answers.

Head to Analyze→Monte Carlo Analysis. You might notice all the other cool optimization tools under the Analyze menu. We'll get to those! First, we need to see where we're at with a preliminary analysis. We've done our best to give the tool accurate information, so here's where the rubber meets the road. Let's give it a whirl!

We came to Monte Carlo analysis first. It's the first one on the menu under Analyze. You may have noticed there's also historical analysis. Let's talk about the different analyses this planning tool does. The simplest is deterministic analysis. This type uses your specified rates of return for your asset classes and the same inflation rate every year for the rest of your life. It's a straight-line analysis; those things don't vary year-to-year like they do in real life. It can act as a baseline, but isn't very useful and certainly not something I'd depend on. The tabular projections and graphical projections we covered in the last chapter are using deterministic analysis. That's why they're called projections. In this phase of our journey, we're trying to see if it's safe to retire, even if the worst economic conditions present themselves.

Monte Carlo analysis is more sophisticated than deterministic because it simulates what happens in real life—rates of return on your various asset classes will vary from year to year. We know that assets that tend to give higher returns on your investments are more volatile, i.e. their standard deviation is higher. More risk, more return, right? Safer investments like bonds don't have those wild swings, but they vary. Pralana has standard deviations for common asset classes built in, but you can enter your own. You want to do this, especially if you're investing in things like alternative investments, crypto, and so forth. Otherwise, use the defaults. There is a checkbox to control this behavior, labeled Use Custom ROR Std Deviations.

There's a button in the upper right labeled "Spending Strategies" and text beneath it telling you what the active spending strategy is. I like to start out with Specified Expenses Only (if yours doesn't say that, go to Analyze→Spending Strategies and change it). This means we'll first do the analysis by seeing if the spending you laid out earlier will work. That's your preferred retirement, right? Later, we'll look at alternative spending strategies.

There's also a checkbox to use correlated asset classes. This means the asset classes you're specifying will tend to move together. For example, one goes up, they all go up. When one goes down, the other correlated ones go down. When the stock market goes down (because people are scared and selling), safe harbors like US Treasury bonds have a tendency to go up, but it's not a guarantee. They are uncorrelated—unrelated. That's because scared people are selling their stocks and looking for safe haven in bonds. It's a simple economic principle—when there's demand for something, the price goes up, when there's a lack of demand, it goes down. Corporate bonds tend to react similar to stocks, because when people lose faith in the stock market, they also lose faith that those corporate bonds will be repaid. It's the same with aggregate bond funds, but not to a large degree, as aggregate funds hold US Treasuries in addition to corporate bonds. Those could be going down just as you need them, which is why I prefer Treasuries in pre-retirement or retirement accounts. If you're using just stocks and bonds, leave this setting off. If you have assets you know are correlated, set it.

TIP: You have the option to view the analysis/graph in today's dollars or future dollars, per the radio button at the top of the page. I recommend starting out in today's dollars, because that's how we're wired to think. It's easier to get your head around the numbers. However, if you're thinking in terms of that final financial asset value the graph is showing, and how much you might leave behind in that year, choose future dollars (although, today's dollars will help you assess that spending power).

When we click the big green Run Monte Carlo Analysis button, the tool's algorithms will do a thousand iterations over your planned spending, income, investment returns, and more to see if there are cases where you could run out of money. It will use your specified inflation rate for things like cost and income increases, and only vary your investment returns, using the standard deviations (volatility) expressed for each of them (you can view these at the Rate of Return Std Deviations tab on this page). The analysis results in a ton of information, but what we're after at a high level is your plan's success rate. This is measured by what percentage of those simulations were successful. For example, if the result is a 92% success rate, your plan could run out of money in 8% of test cases. These are most likely the ones where longer sequences of poor investment returns happened. This is more damaging when it occurs early in retirement, and is called sequence of returns risk, or simply "sequence risk."

TIP: The gold standard to shoot for is a success rate of 90% or more. Why not 100%? If you hit 100%, we know the plan never fails under the simulations, that's good. But, it could also mean it is overly conservative, possibly meaning things like assets piling up and causing a tax bomb, or simply living too conservatively and hence much life unlived. If we see rates in the 90s, we know we're right at the sweet spot. That small failure risk is often easily mitigated by normal human behavior during those long economic downturns—we cut back a little on spending. However, if one or both of you are very risk averse, or have spending control issues, you might want to at least start out at 100%.

Let's see what the case is for good old Dick and Jane. They've probably grown impatient waiting, with all this blathering going on. After pressing the button to run the analysis (a thousand iterations in 20 seconds!). The resulting information appears. We see the green rainbow graph toward the top that says "100% Success." The table to the right lists their success rate for their final ten years as 100% in each year. Amazing, right? Don't pop the champagne corks just yet. When I run the analysis with clients and see 100% success rates, I tell them they're either working too long, maybe not spending enough money, or both!

TIP: Defer to the rainbow success graph, which is the overall success percentage, and then the final ten years success rate. A plan could fail earlier in worse case scenarios but recover to 100% in the last ten years in the better percentiles.

The deterministic and Monte Carlo final savings are shown above the graph. This is what the tool projects you may pass away with. Remember, it doesn't include property, and it's in today's dollars. I ask clients, "Is that how much you intend to leave behind?" Typically, the answer is, "No! We love our kids, but not that much. They'll get the house. We're spending our hard-earned money." There's a feature in the tool to fix that problem, and we'll get to it.

Let's focus on the pretty graph. There's a solid red line that shows the deterministic result. That's the fixed analysis we talked about earlier. There are a series of blue bands that represent the percentile results of randomized rates of return variations. The worst financial outcomes are modeled by the lower and lightest blue bands. If those ever touch bottom, it represents you running out of money. The higher light blue bands represent the outcomes in the best financial circumstances, the "blue sky" results. The darkest blue band is the 40th to 60th percentile result, and the most likely circumstance to occur. Look to the left, along the horizontal axis, to see what your projected ending balance is for any of those bands.

There's also a dashed red line that shows expenses over your years remaining. You can turn this off to get it out of the way, if you just want to focus on savings. Look for any spikes up or down and make sure you understand them. Dick and Jane have a big one around 2042—the year they intend to sell their home. That can be an expensive event with closing costs, moving costs, and so forth. You can zoom in on any section of the graph by clicking the zoom icon in the upper right, and then selecting an area to view.

I pay close attention to the trajectory of the graph. Remember, when we're working, we're in asset accumulation phase. We're supposed to be saving for retirement (and much more)! But, when we retire, we're supposed to enter asset enjoyment mode—enjoying all the money we worked hard for all those decades, working on that bucket list of things we dreamed about as we trudged off to work each day. This is the biggest mental shift people have trouble with. It's really hard, after drilling "save, save, save" into your brain for all those years. The result is a graph like the one we're seeing for Dick and Jane. The lines are all trending upward as they get older. They're staying in asset accumulation mode! If you are truly in asset decumulation/enjoyment mode, the graph should trend downward, signifying life lived, money enjoyed. If you want to continue to grow your assets, perhaps to generously give upon your death, or just be very conservative, this is fine. We'll work to solve that problem in the next chapter!

> NOTE: The graph is showing the value of your financial assets over time, not your net worth! This doesn't include any property you have.

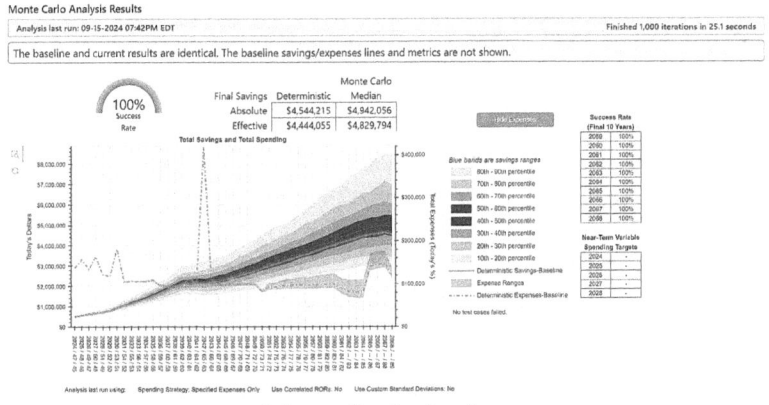

Monte Carlo Analysis

> NOTE: Don't fret if your plan didn't result in success rates above 90%. This is a preliminary trial run! There are tons of ways to optimize and better the results, and we'll explore them later in this book.

Historical Analysis

Head to Analyze→Historical Analysis. We have the Activate Historical Sequence Analysis and Use CAPE Strategy check boxes off for now. Before we run the analysis, click the tab labeled Historical Rates of Return and Inflation. In the first tab, Historical Asset Classes and Inflation, we see a series of tabular data starting with the year 1928. The returns are listed in each year for the S&P 500 (representing the stocks asset class), 10-Year Treasury Bonds (representing intermediate-term bonds), 3-Month Treasury Bonds (short-term bonds), and Cash. The remaining two columns contain the inflation rate for each year and the CAPE ratio. You can even specify your own custom datasets for other types of assets, but it's a very advanced use case rabbit hole that we won't be going down in this book. The user manual covers that in great detail.

> NOTE: The CAPE ratio is essentially a financial metric that is used to project whether a stock (or, in this case, the stock market) is overvalued. The idea is that if the market is overvalued, we're due for a correction, meaning stock values will drop. It's been a bellwether of market downturns. Because of this, some planners prefer to tie their success results and even spending to the CAPE. Yet, this is a good example of sliding into the behavior of trying to time the market. When you do that, you will almost always be wrong.

I've explained how Monte Carlo analysis works. In contrast, historical analysis iterates over your plan and replicates those historical asset returns and inflation for each year of your projected lifespan, starting with the first year of results available, which is 1928. This will continue for as long as possible. Obviously, with almost a hundred years of data available, and anyone doing this planning being unlikely to live another hundred years, that will be limited. See the detailed description in the Pralana help file, with the examples stated there, to understand in more detail.

The upshot is that past economic trends will be replicated over your plan going forward from the current plan start year to see what the impact will be. That includes events like the Great Depression, 1999 Dot-Com Bust, and late-2000s Great Recession. While it is interesting to see if your retirement would have survived those economic catastrophes, I'm not sure it's all that relevant. For example, when the stock market crashed in the fall of 1929 to kick off the Great Depression, there was nothing to stop the market from falling—only that closing bell at the end of the trading day. It kept falling and falling, out of control. We learned our lesson! Since then, we have circuit breakers that will stop trading if that sort of thing occurs, giving everyone a chance to take a breather and stop panicking.

Theoretically, that can't occur again. Same with the other controls and mitigations we've installed after the other events. The COVID crisis was the ultimate black-swan event—almost overnight, most of the world was out of work. Supply chains ground to a halt, all commerce effectively ground to a halt. It was a thing far worse than the Great Depression, and should have resulted in economic disaster for decades. But it didn't, because of the miraculous steps we took. We used loans and stimulus payments to keep households, businesses, and the stock and bond markets afloat. The Federal Reserve bought bonds. The inescapable high inflation from that kind of event occurred, but we've (so far!) done a wonderful job at taming it without causing a recession. And by the way, you might think the worst time to have retired would have been on the cusp of the Great Depression or COVID. It wasn't! It was around 1965, the beginning of a very long recessionary period of super high interest rates, inflation, unemployment, and stock market doldrums.

We never want to be overly confident, but my point is to take historical analysis with a grain of salt. It can be useful. For example, I've had clients who didn't believe in bonds. "The money is all in the stock market. Why would I have bonds?" This can be dangerous when the timeframe for needing the money is near, such as near or in retirement, because of the sequence risk we've discussed. I've found I can best show that sequence risk by using historical analysis. I'll show you how shortly, but first, let's cover the basics.

> TIP: We do see a common relationship between interest rates and stock/bond prices. When the Federal Reserve raises interest rates, it's considered "bad for business" as consumers are less likely to take out loans to buy homes and vehicles. So, the stock market typically drops on this news. However, with higher interest rates, bonds will yield more, and investors will move to those safe havens. In related behavior, existing bonds that now have lower interest rates than those that can currently be bought aren't attractive, and if sold, must be sold at a discount to their par value. All of this happens in reverse when the Fed cuts interest rates!

We'll start with today's dollars and click the Run Historical Analysis button for Dick and Jane (who have been waiting patiently). The analysis again shows a 100% success rate, however, this time the page shows a table of best and worst years they would have fared under. We see that ominous 1965 in the worst years, as usual! The historical analysis median ending balance is about two million dollars more than the one from the Monte Carlo analysis as well. This leads us to believe that historical analysis may be overly optimistic.

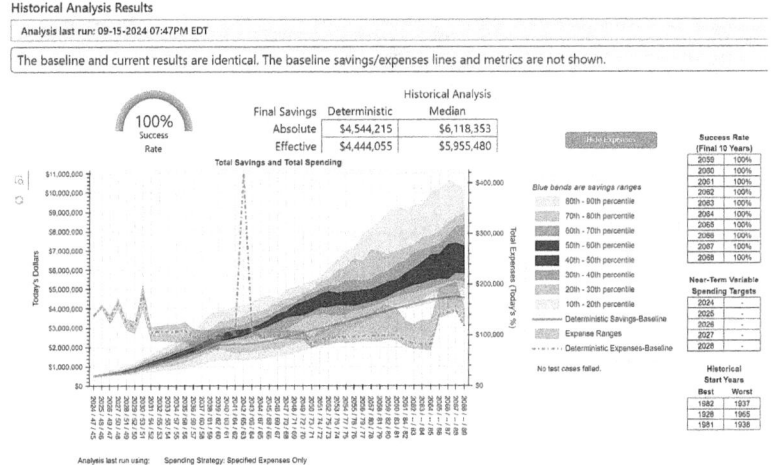

Historical Analysis

Historical Sequence Analysis

There's a great feature in the planning tool that would let you see exactly how you'd fare if one of the economic disasters we mentioned happened during your life. You can check the box Activate Historical Sequence Analysis and provide the year you want to start with—for example, 1965 for those most dire circumstances. This provides a new orange-yellow line on your graph to show the impact on your financial assets. This is how I show those overzealous stock-investing clients how sequence risk can cause them to run out of money.

Let's check the box and enter 1965 as the year to start. The graph refreshes and we see the yellow-orange lines to represent what a 1965-like economic trend would do to Dick and Jane's financial life. Wow, the long period of stagnation in that era shows itself clearly here! Dick and Jane's financial assets are essentially flat-lined up into the 2050s. It's reassuring, because it never actually dips lower, on a downward trajectory, and certainly never bottoms out to zero, which would mean plan failure. We want the graph to trend lower, but not for that reason! It can be fun (or scary!) to put in the start years for other periods, like the 2008 financial crisis. It can also be a good way to reassure a nervous spouse or partner. That's the beauty of building a reliable, high-fidelity financial roadmap—it often results in permission to spend, permission to enjoy life.

> TIP: If you're going to retire in ten years and want to see what would happen if 1965-like conditions occurred at the start of your retirement, simply use 1965 as the starting year for Historical Sequence Analysis.

You'll notice a lime-green warning box in the upper right of the browser window that historical sequence analysis is activated. When we covered the tabular projections, I informed you that the tabular results use straight-line deterministic numbers. When you've activated historical sequence analysis, those tabular projection numbers will change to reflect those results, not the pure deterministic ones. The warning is there because it's easy to check out the historical consequences, then forget the checkbox is on, and later make poor decisions (for example, withdrawals) based on those numbers. OK, uncheck the Historical Sequence Analysis box now, before you forget!

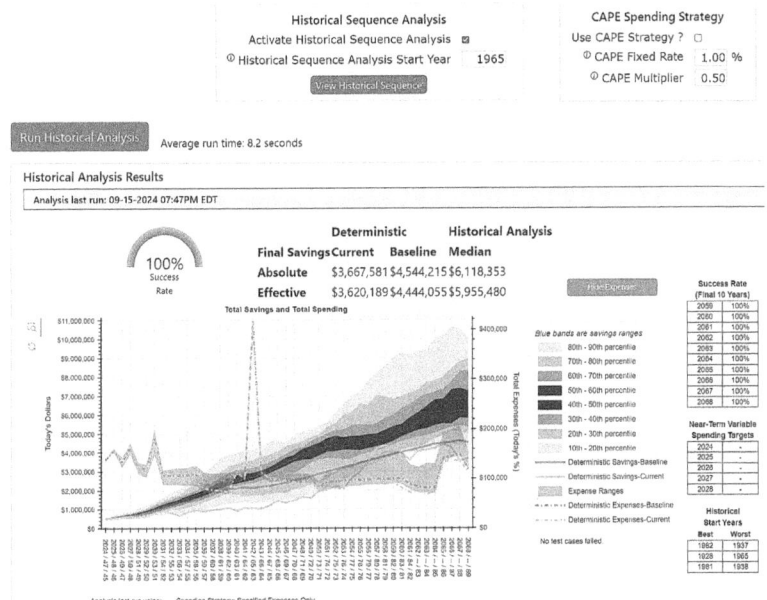

Historical Sequence Analysis

We've determined through deterministic (flat-line), Monte Carlo, and historical analysis that Dick and Jane are just fine. Maybe too fine! Let's move on to some optimization steps.

CHAPTER NINE

OPTIMIZE FOR THE WIN

NOT QUITE THERE? HERE'S HOW TO CROSS THE FINISH LINE

WHETHER OR NOT YOUR plan shows acceptable success rates, you should still optimize. We want every dollar you've worked hard for, or thoughtful people have left behind for you, to be enjoyed. We want to practice tax avoidance (the legal kind), not tax evasion (the illegal kind). You paid into systems like Social Security (SS) all your working life. Let's make sure you get the maximum benefit! Some of these optimizations should be done in a particular order, as the results will affect each other. I'll say again, don't start this process unless you're very sure your plan is complete and accurate.

Social Security Optimization

Head to Analyze→Optimize Social Security Start Age. You might first check to be very sure you've entered your projected benefit at full retirement age (FRA) on the page at Build→Income→Social

Security. Otherwise, this will all be meaningless. It's a common mistake for folks to determine they want to claim at a certain age, and enter their benefit at that age into the tool. No. You need to enter your FRA unless you're currently receiving benefits (in which case, that's the number you enter, and really there's nothing to optimize here except perhaps a spouse).

> TIP: There are many Social Security optimization sites and tools on the internet. However, they don't have the complete context of your financial details that the one in Pralana has. For that reason, I avoid them unless trying to get an answer to a very particular question. They may show you how to get every dollar out of the Social Security system, but you may lose out in other ways, such as higher taxes in the long run because of the impact on things like Roth conversion tax rates or IRA required minimum distributions.

Dick and Jane didn't know what to put, so they went with the standard go-to of saying they'll collect at full retirement age, which is 67 for both of them. Running the optimizer, we see a much better path forward—Jane starting SS at age 64 and 11 months (earlier than age 67), and Dick starting at age 69 and 9 months (later than age 67). The extra money, $127,475, this will yield them is about enough to buy a beautiful RV or small cabin somewhere! Granted, most of the savings will come over time, later in life. But, still!

TIP: You might also choose to set your Social Security claiming age(s) to 70 (the latest it would make sense to wait, as there's no benefit growth after that other than for inflation) and do the Roth conversion optimizer first, to see what it comes up with when SS income is off the table. This might benefit folks with almost all their nest egg in pretax, and it's a sizeable amount. It could also be run as a separate scenario. The same would hold true for pensions or other pretax income-type payments you can choose to defer payments on.

The optimizer shows a grid with different claiming ages. There's a blue dot to show what you had chosen earlier. The green circle with a black outline shows the sweet spot. There may be other green circles that are also very good, and close to the optimal result. You can hover over the different dots and areas to see what the difference is in claiming at various ages. There's a Use Optimized Ages button to accept the optimized ages and set them for you under Build→Income→Social Security. Dick and Jane say, "Heck, yeah!" and take that win.

TIP: If you don't need the Social Security income, some will say to take it and invest the money. However, if you feel your market returns will beat the bump in your payment from waiting, don't forget to factor in the taxable income the SS will generate. It can affect your ability to do Roth conversions and much more. Some prefer to just let it ride until age 70, as the ultimate inflation-adjusted pension and insurance against bad economic times and/or long-term care expenses late in life.

Pralana Gold has a sensitivities feature that allows metrics like SS claiming age to be tweaked up and down without changing your actual plan inputs. As of this writing, it's not yet implemented in Pralana Online. In my experience using that with clients, they've always been surprised to find it doesn't make a lot of difference when they claim SS (aside from major impacts on needed Roth conversions). After all, the mathematicians at the SS administration work hard to level things out so that no matter when you claim, you end up receiving about the same amount of money. The benefits of waiting are often blown out of proportion by click-bait articles. It's important to factor things like longevity and health when making this decision. When shown the minor difference in their payments granted by waiting, and that the apex point where it pays off dollar-wise (usually mid-late 80s), clients often say, "What the heck will I do with the money then?" However, if you don't have a big nest egg, or other income sources such as pensions, and will rely heavily on SS for your retirement success, it's often better to wait if you can afford to.

> TIP: Always remember, this isn't so much about money and math as it is about happiness. We want to make sound money decisions, but you should lead with, "What will make us happier?" and then see if the math supports it. Don't waste your remaining time on this blue marble chasing every dollar. Don't forget to have fun and enjoy every sandwich[1].

---

1. After being diagnosed with terminal lung cancer at age 55, musician Warren Zevon appeared on the David Letterman show. In the heartbreaking interview, he was asked his advice to others, given his now short life expectancy. "Enjoy every sandwich," was his reply. Slow down, enjoy the things that really matter.

Roth Conversion Optimization

Here's another personal finance/planning tactic that's often blown way out of proportion. I'm not bashing it—it can be a powerful tool to avoid taxes and build tax-free assets. The math will tell us whether it's a good idea from that perspective. This is another one of those areas where you should consider the emotional/happiness reasons in context with the math. For example, some people do Roth conversions in order to shield their spouse from the potential of paying that widow/widower tax (single taxpayer rate) should they pass earlier than expected. This factors into May-December couples where there's a large age disparity, or when one spouse has poor health and perhaps a shorter expected timeline. Some people do the conversions because they want to pass the money on to heirs tax-free. Often, by the time we pass, our kids are in their prime earning years and in a high tax bracket already. Passing them a pretax account means they'll give a lot of that money you wanted them to have to Uncle Sam instead, and perhaps push them into an even higher tax rate on their job income. Finally, you might do conversions in order to stay ahead of future tax hikes. Our country is in a lot of debt, and that piper has to be paid at some point.

It's a good strategy to consider these moves late in the year, when your tax picture is almost final. You have those last or next-to-last paystubs to work from, realized capital gain info from your brokerage, and lots of other info. Use a good tax planning tool to determine your marginal tax rate and consider topping off any room left in that rate (or the next higher one) with a conversion. Pay the taxes out of pocket (with your tax return in April). Avoid using the converted dollars to pay taxes as they're golden dollars that will grow tax free in your Roth account. If you're absolutely sure you'll convert a certain amount, an alternate strategy is to convert if there's a big market drop during the year, and let those shares recover tax free on the rebound. Also, don't go too crazy—if you anticipate long-term care expenses, you'd want to pay them from your pretax IRA as they typically provide a nice tax deduction late in life. Also, don't optimize away any monies for charity, especially after age 70 1/2 when you can use them as Qualified Charitable Distributions.

Click on Analyze→Roth Conversions in the menu. To get started, I recommend disabling Roth conversions using the radio button at the top, then running another Monte Carlo simulation. This establishes your baseline with no conversions being done. Come back to the Roth conversions page. If there are rows under the table at the top, delete all but one row and use it to set your preferred starting point. For example, you might specify the current year as the starting year, proportional as the priority, something like 22% TCJA and 25% Post-TCJA as the maximum income tax rate, 15% as the maximum LTCG rate. If you're on Medicare, you might set an IRMAA limit, and the same with the FPL for any Affordable Care Act (ACA) subsidies you may be receiving.

I'd recommend leaving those settings alone for now and seeing what the optimizer comes up with, and whether is will affect your Medicare and ACA payments, and go from there. I've seen too many cases where people freak out about a small increase in very affordable health care premiums and forego large benefits in reduced taxation and free growth! ACA subsidies tend to be highest above two times the federal poverty level (FPL), so that might be a good limit to set when doing Roth conversions. Again, don't cut off your nose to spite your face—the conversions may provide a better benefit over the rest of your life!

Let's do this. Hit the Optimize Roth Conversions button. When it completes, the first thing that catches our eye is the Active vs Baseline graph. Our baseline is no conversions (in blue) and the best result the optimizer could come up with is shown with a red line. The actual numbers are in a table below this. It's important to pay attention to both. For example, the numbers may show there's a large dollar benefit to doing the recommended conversions. However, if the graph shows a marked difference in spendable income throughout your prime years (because of paying the taxes on the conversions each year) and the ROI crossover point where you actually reap the benefit is close to your projected expiration, you may think twice.

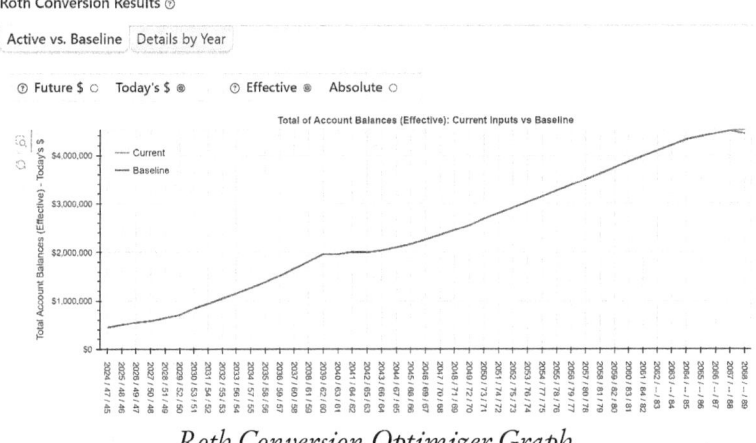

Roth Conversion Optimizer Graph

	Total of Final Account Balances		Total Fed/ State/Local
	Absolute	Effective	Tax
Current Inputs	4,635,310	4,530,694	1,025,808
Baseline Inputs	4,544,215	4,444,055	1,016,721
Change	91,095	86,639	9,087

(Values show are in today's $)

Roth Conversion Optimizer Table

The optimizer finds little to no benefit for Dick and Jane. If we click on the Details by Year tab, there are just a few small conversions recommended from each of their accounts later in life, when they're around retirement. The numbers in the table show that doing the recommended conversions will add $91,095 absolute and $86,639 effective to their wealth over the rest of their lives, and save them $9,087 in taxes. If you check the graph, the two lines (representing conversions vs no conversions) overlap each other until the last few years of their lives. That's when the $9,087 payoff comes. Not very motivating! That said, It's nothing to sneeze at, but certainly not huge numbers. Why? We thought Roth conversions were the bomb!

I'll tell you why. If you look at their taxes in the tabular projections or graphical projections, you'll see Dick and Jane really don't have a tax problem. Their effective tax rate over the rest of their lives is projected to be in the teens, and they eek into the 25% marginal in some years, 10-15% in others. If you check their accounts they're not sitting on a massive amount of pretax money, there's no "tax bomb" waiting for them when they reach required minimum distribution age. Another factor that might cause sub-par Roth conversion recommendations is when you're showing that you're just not spending the money—you don't need it, so why pay taxes on those conversions? Leave it to the heirs (evil laugh). Which again, goes to the non-mathematical reasons to convert—pay taxes for heirs, help a spouse avoid the higher widow/widower single tax rates, and insulate yourself from future higher tax rates (including the 2017 TCJA expiration at the end of 2025).

In this tab, you can also see the impact on ACA subsidies and lots of tax info. If you're planning to follow the recommendations, make sure you're looking at the amounts in future dollars! The sequence list at the top has also changed, to reflect what the optimizer is recommending and why. You'll see that it replaced our default 22%/25% income tax max with some conversions in years that will top off the 10%/10% and 12%/15% brackets. That's a pretty good deal.

> NOTE: If you're using Asset Allocation Mode 1, read the online help for examples of how that mode specifically works with Roth conversion optimization. Find that at Build→Financial Assets→Advanced Portfolio Modeling→Asset Allocation/Location.

In reviewing this information with Dick and Jane, I'd advise them to do the late-year tax analysis each early December, and perhaps just top off their marginal bracket with conversions. I'd also urge them to consider those non-math reasons for doing them and make the decision that they both agree on. You may see some weirdness, where the tool is doing conversions well above the amount that would affect your ACA subsidies or Medicare IRMAA. This could happen because something else already drove your AGI above those levels, so the tool says, "Welp, they're already blown past that, so let's go full speed ahead on conversions!"

> TIP: Check out the Review→Tabular Projections→Expenses→Taxes→AGI Detail results. Each Roth conversion is hyperlinked with a pop-up that gives the rationale behind the constraints and why the planning tool calculated that value as optimum.

One last thing. As Dick and Jane have accepted the few measly conversions that were recommended, we want to lock those into their base scenario analysis. Head back to Analyze→Monte Carlo Analysis. There's an orange line on the graph for the deterministic (fixed-rate) savings and expenses. This reflects changes that were made since the last analysis run. It's nice, because you can see the effect of any changes you've made. If you run the analysis again, those orange lines will disappear, as the changes are now incorporated.

Optimize Withdrawal Priorities

Let's investigate Analyze→Optimize Withdrawal Priorities. This is a powerful feature! It is essentially calculating where to draw any needed funds from your nest egg each year, in order to minimize taxes and thus maximize your potential savings. It's one of those things you really can't do on your own. The tool considers your cash floor preference, as well as sources of income, to meet your expense needs. When it perceives a "cash shortage" in your checking/savings, it knows it needs to withdraw from other accounts. This is why you see some text showing years there are "cash shortages." It doesn't mean you've run out of money, just that you've run down to the floor of your checking/savings. It's another reason it's so important to establish those floor and ceiling values in Build→Financial Assets→Management→Cash Floor and Ceiling.

Some years it may be better to lean on your brokerage, other years from the Roth, other years from pretax accounts. It lays out that withdrawal roadmap for you to follow for the rest of your life. Once you know the numbers, it becomes very easy to work the bucket system (if you're following that technique) and set up monthly autopilot transfers from the desired account to your checking for the upcoming year. Keep in mind, this will not override any scheduled withdrawals you already have set up.

This is also a very simple tool to run. Just press the button! Doing so for Dick and Jane reveals a table of results (in future dollars), and, you guessed it, a graph. The numbers show that optimizing their withdrawal order has earned Dick and Jane another $14,363, so they'll press the Adopt Optimized Withdrawal Priority button. Wait! Where did the optimized withdrawal roadmap go? You can see it at Build→Financial Assets→Management→Withdrawal Priorities. If you want to see the actual withdrawals by dollar from each account per year, head to Review→Tabular Projections→Cash Flow→Withdrawals. This is your lifetime withdrawal roadmap. It's very useful for setting up your annual buckets! Heading back to Analyze→Monte Carlo Analysis, we see that orange line again, so we'll re-run the analysis to lock this change in.

Earliest Safe Retirement Age

With that, we're pretty optimized-out. But, we still have work to do! Remember back when we first saw those golden 100% success rates for Dick and Jane? I mentioned my favorite line, "You're either working too long, or maybe not spending enough, or both!" I promised to revisit that question, and here we are. Head to Analyze→Earliest Safe Retirement Analysis. This tool will calculate the earliest date one can retire (or both if married). You can't pick one person if you've indicated you're married. It's going to run more Monte Carlo simulations to find the earliest date that still results on a success rate at or above 90% (if there is one!). Let's press the green Run Earliest Safe Retirement Analysis button and give it a whirl.

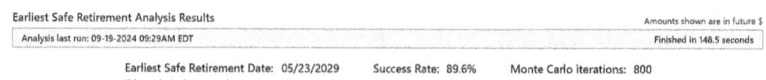

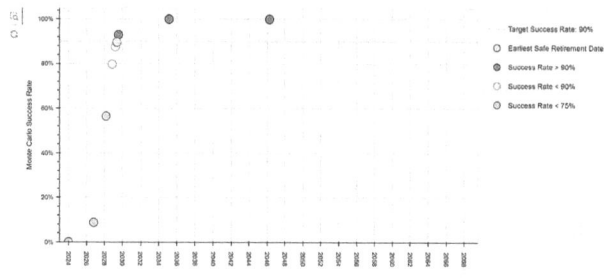

Earliest Safe Retire Date

Happy day, Dick and Jane! You can ***both*** retire far earlier than expected, in May of 2029 rather than the planned years of 2041 and 2043. The tool has done another 800 Monte Carlo iterations (it will vary based on need) and comes up with a success rate of 90.6% There goes Dick's dreams of heading to the ol' fishing hole for two years while Jane slogs off to her final years of work! It's good to hear this, but in reality, many people will still go off to work knowing that they don't have to be there. It's quite liberating! I mentioned earlier that the FIRE community is really more interested in that financial independence than relegating to the front porch rocking chair at 45 years old.

> NOTE: Not to be a Debbie Downer, but remember that if your retirement date is reliant on certain intangibles, like vesting in pension, health care, or other benefits, factor those into this good news.

The graph results allow you to research different dates, in case you don't want to go with the optimized one. Maybe Dick or Jane are skeptical, but willing to compromise at 95%. You can find that date in the graph as well. If they jump the gun and retire a year earlier in 2028, their success rate drops to 56.5%. Be patient, Dick and Jane!

Spending Strategies

Let's tackle the other half of that blue-sky equation. Assume Dick and Jane don't want to retire earlier. They'll stick with their pre-planned dates (we'll see about that!). They've turned to the other question—how much more can we spend in retirement? When we did our initial analysis, we stuck with their specified expenses. We'd like to answer the question, "How much more can Dick and Jane spend if they stick to their retirement date, and still stay at or above that magic 90% threshold?"

Consumption Smoothing

On the Analysis→Spending Strategies page, we find a bulleted list of possibilities. Specified Expenses Only is the first choice, and we covered that. Let's select Consumption Smoothing. Note that we can choose Deterministic, Monte Carlo, or Historical. We've covered the pros and cons of each approach. Let's start with Monte Carlo and see what that says. After spinning the wheel, we see that Dick and Jane can spend another $56,416 per year starting with this year (the plan start year), and have a 91% chance of success. Hey now! That's a few nice vacations per year, for sure. As usual, the graph below allows you to find compromises.

To test this, Dick and Jane could simply plug in another $56,416 in vacation spending each year, re-run the Monte Carlo analysis, and they should see results around 90% (keep in mind, we're running random simulations, so the results will never be exactly the same two runs in a row).

> TIP: Many clients I work with love seeing these numbers, but often prefer to take the knowledge with a grain of salt and spend as planned in their first few retirement years. They'll wait and see if the money piles up and then adopt the additional spending with confidence.

Also, keep in mind that these results will be sticky, i.e. there's no "adopt" button as there was in Pralana Gold/Excel and as we've seen in other places in Pralana Online. These changes are kept as long as you keep consumption smoothing as your spending strategy. If we go back to the Monte Carlo Analysis page and view the graph, we see a big change. Remember that problematic upward moving lines that show Dick and Jane are still in asset accumulation, no-fun mode throughout their lives? Now we see a yellow line that reflects our change to consumption smoothed spending. It's a much more reasonable trajectory for retired people, basically flat-lining but never quite hitting zero. The dashed line for expenses is, of course, higher.

Let's run it again, this time with Historical analysis. Change the radio button and re-run. Voila, the historical approach yields additional spending of $43,115 and 89.6% success. That's not surprising, as we're analyzing spending, and if you recall, inflation variability is factored in with historical analysis (it is not with Monte Carlo). For that reason, I'm more of a fan of historical analysis for consumption smoothing. If you decide you're going to accept the guidance and do additional spending, perhaps take that number and reasonably allocate it across your phased, miscellaneous, and non-QCD charitable giving. After you do that, change your spending strategy back to specified expenses, since now it's all baked in.

> TIP: Consumption smoothing can also work in the other direction. Suppose your plan analysis has you at 85% success—not quite enough, by our standards. If you run consumption smoothing, it will show you how much you need to cut spending to get over the hump!

Other Spending Strategies

I'm not as much a fan of the remaining spending strategies, except for one. Let's do a quick survey of them, and I'll explain my reasons.

Constant Spending—This is for implementing something like the 4% Rule, as discussed in Chapter 2. You specify a starting percentage, and it's bumped up each year based on the previous year's inflation, to keep your spending power level. But, a tool like this is merely projecting or using historical inflation. You'd want to do that based on actual inflation.

Fixed % Spending—This allows you to specify to always spend a specific percentage of your remaining savings. Again, the tool can only project that based on simulations.

Fixed % with Floor and Ceiling—This is the same as above, but with a hard floor and ceiling established on your spending amounts.

Guyton-Klinger—Much discussed in financial articles, and kind of cool, but still the same problem of relying on projections rather than the actual data the real method calls for.

Target Percentage Adjustment—This differs from fixed percent spending above in that you state you want to spend a certain percentage of your starting savings amount, not a percent of what it is each year as you go forward (remaining savings).

Actuarial Spending—Ah, now this one solves a long-standing problem! You specify a legacy amount, meaning how much you want to leave behind to heirs, and then run the Monte Carlo or Historical analysis. Although most of my clients answer this question with, "Whatever is left," or "Just the property," some have a number in mind. This may hold true for blended second marriages, where each spouse has only children from their former marriage. This is why I suggested that after running consumption smoothing, incorporate the numbers into your plan. That allows you to come back here and then work on baking in a legacy amount, if that's your wish. It will probably push you below 90%, so then adjust spending as needed to get back there.

TIP: Leaving money behind. We just showed how you can use the actuarial spending strategy to accomplish this. You may want more granularity, for example, specifying an account, or percentage. You can also specify that you're buying an annuity without showing any payout. That disappears the money from the account at the designated time with no tax consequences. You can also insert a scheduled withdrawal from the accounts for the year you expect this to happen. It will be taxed if it's a pretax account, unless you make it a charitable contribution, which you can do on the charity page as a QCD.

CAPE—You'll find this one on the regular historical analysis page, not here. It's complex and requires a few tricky parameters to run. I've already said that CAPE has been a pretty reliable metric for determining stocks are overvalued, we're in a bubble, and a correction may be looming. But again, we don't know what future CAPE values will be, so we can only model the past.

Post Optimization Notes

If you've done everything we've discussed so far, and your plan still doesn't hit the 90% success mark, what next? There are a few things to consider.

- When you did the consumption smoothing, it should have recommended a decrease in spending to get you to 90%. Look at your expenses. Can you make that happen somewhere without sacrificing your quality of life to an unacceptable level?

- Is it possible you can work just a little longer (per what the safe retirement date suggested), or perhaps monetize one of your passions with a part-time side hustle? Kiss Your Money Hello has a whole chapter on ideas! Perhaps remediate debt as well, which KYMH can also help with. Interest charges can really your future. Is it viable in the current interest rate environment to refinance your mortgage?

- Are you too conservatively invested? Keep your own risk tolerance capacity in mind, but does tweaking your asset allocation toward stocks more help make up the difference? Always keep the bucket strategy we discussed in mind, and ensure any money you need in the next five years isn't in the market.

- Are you comfortable with less than a 90% success rate? I've had clients that are, because they feel they're financially responsible and would cut back on spending should hard economic times happen. Advisors, planners, and the tools shoot for 90% but it's a personal decision.

Of course, when a new year is starting, you're well armed with a lot of this information as you set up your plan or update it for the new year. You'll put in your year-starting balances, so any damage done or victories won (financially) in the past year will be baked in as the new starting point for our analysis going forward. As I have these meetings with clients, the past always comes up. If it's been a bad series of years, they always get nervous and want to scale back a bit. That's what these more complicated methods (Monte Carlo and historical simulations) are trying to model, but it's also human nature to be fearful. And let's not forget, poor performance is already baked into the tool, the simulations, and the results! If your analysis passes all those up and down Monte Carlo simulations, and all those horrible past historical economic circumstances, bad stuff is already baked in, rest easy.

TIP: If you want to enter Roth conversions manually, just head to Build→Financial Assets→Scheduled Withdrawals and enter the withdrawal from your tax deferred account. Then head to Build→Income→Employment and enter a personal contribution to a Roth in one of your income streams (create one if you don't have one). Make sure to set the optimizer to do no conversion for that year if you want to use it for other years.

At this point, we're optimized out! You might go to Review→Tabular Projections→Expenses→Taxes, scroll down the list of IRA withdrawal years for your effective tax rate, take an average, then re-enter the amount in Build→Financial Assets→Management→Effective Tax Rate. Remember back when we took a guestimate and said we'd circle back? Now is that time. When changes are made to the plan, I typically go through the same routine. Optimize Social Security, then Roth conversions, then withdrawal order, then spending.

Your base scenario is done! If you're still not quite there, consider the advice in Kiss Your Money Hello[2] to shore up your financial situation in general, including strategies to pay down debt and increase income. I'd take a moment to back up your data and print input, output reports, and some key tabular data and graphs. Then go have a nice meal together!

---

2. https://books2read.com/kissyourmoneyhello

Chapter Ten

Swizzle Up Some Scenarios

What If and Whatnot

When I'm working with clients, by this point they're pretty excited. Most times, they're finding they're in far better shape than they had dared to dream. Sometimes, they're excited to at least now know where they stand, and ready to work to get things to where they want them. They've seen the light at the end of the tunnel, and finally it's not an oncoming train! This is when the ideas happen. "Hey, maybe we can buy that vacation home, boat or RV!" "Hey, maybe we can move to a warmer, sunnier state!"

If these are simply pie-in-the-sky dreams at this point, create an alternate scenario to test them out. You get three scenarios to work with in Pralana Online. You might think you can check a move to a new state easily in Build→Get Started→Scenario Assumptions and the Residence/Location tab. Just add a new row and year, right? Not so simple. There's a lot more involved—you have to factor in the sale of your existing home, purchase of a new one, or the related expenses if renting. You'll have moving costs as well. Some people use the other two scenarios to create an optimistic outlook for things we need to project, such as inflation and market returns, and a pessimistic outlook for those. You could use a scenario to factor in things like an inheritance that you're not sure enough about to put in your base scenario. The varieties are endless. Use your imagination!

Now that Dick and Jane have their base scenario complete, and they know they're in very good shape, they're thinking, "What the hay, let's retire earlier, move to Hawaii, and buy that house and boat we've always dreamed about! John will be done with college and Sue will be almost done. Empty nest!" Uh-oh. Well, maybe it's possible. Let's find out!

> TIP: This is a good time to back up your data and run your input and output reports to a downloaded PDF. It's a good idea to save your stuff before making any major change in computer-land. We'll talk about backing up in the next chapter, and it can be a good way to undo mistakes or get back to a desired place.

In the upper right of the planning tool, there's an icon with a solid square over an outline of a square. If you hover over it, the tag says, "Copy Inputs." (You will only see this if you have more than one scenario defined at Build→Scenario Assumptions→Add/Delete Scenarios.) When we click that, a screen appears with some choices. This capability is far more functional than the old versions, which only allowed for copying Scenario 1 to Scenario 2 or 3. Now we can copy all sorts of ways! That can also be enough rope to hang us, if we're not careful. Note the cautionary note on this page that there's no undo. They're not kidding!

We're going to copy from Scenario 1 to Scenario 2, and we select all items. The ability to do a granular copy here is also a fantastic feature, but we're going for the whole enchilada, and then make our changes. After we double and triple check our settings and press the copy button, a green success message appears. Let's make sure everything went well, and we have two identical scenarios at this point.

TIP: From this point on, you have to be very careful any time you make a change or view any results. Be careful and intentional about which scenario you're working with. It's very easy to make a mistake. Create a constant habit of checking the scenario underline in the upper right to verify which one is current. I recommend working with one scenario at a time when you sit down to work with Pralana, one scenario per session. When you have your main scenario, if that turns out to be Scenario 2 or 3, think about copying it to Scenario 1 (be aware it will overlay whatever is there currently) to always make Scenario 1 your go-to.

Head to the Monte Carlo analysis page. Check the upper right to ensure you are in Scenario 2. If not, click the radio button in the upper left to select it. Run the analysis. Don't be tempted to do anything else! When it's done, let's make use of the one optimization tool we haven't used yet—Analyze→Scenario Analysis Comparisons. The red lines for Scenario 1 and blue lines for Scenario 2 should essentially overlay each other, making purple, in both graphs. Keep in mind that because of the randomness built into Monte Carlo, there will be slight differences.

Next, let's clearly label what Scenario 2 is about. We'll go to Build→Get Started→Scenario Assumptions and the Add/Delete Scenarios tab. I'll label Scenario 2 "2025 HI, House, Boat" and add the note, "Let's go crazy!" We'll make the following changes, taking care that we're making them in Scenario 2!

- Change their retirement date to 12/31/2031, and residence state to Hawaii in 2032

- Change the sell year for the primary home to 2031, and the buy date for the next home to 2032, at a price of $800,000 (a small price for Hawaii!) with a $500,000 15-year mortgage at 5% (Oh, no! Don't go back into debt in retirement, Dick and Jane!)

- Add a miscellaneous expense of $10,000 in 2032 for the move to Hawaii

- Also, as they say in the movie, "You're going to need a bigger boat." They change their previous $75k sailboat purchase to $100k in 2032.

When the numbers are plugged in, Monte Carlo analysis reveals they now have only a 64% chance of success. If we turn the historical sequence analysis on and set it to 1965, they go broke. Uh-oh! If you have to be homeless, I guess Hawaii is a nice place. Dick and Jane calm down, reconsider going back into debt in retirement, and being so far away from family and friends. They decide to take an annual trip to Hawaii instead, using the extra money the consumption smoothing revealed they can spend! Whew, crisis averted.

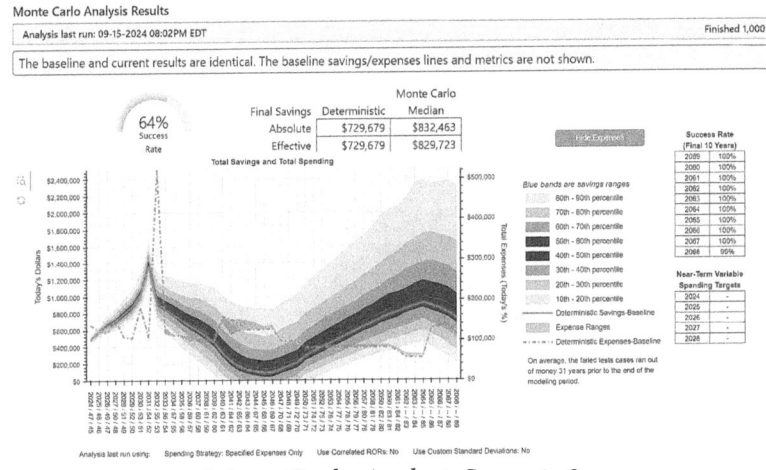

Monte Carlo Analysis Scenario 2

Now back on Earth, they discuss a more legitimate concern—what if they live longer than they expect? Let's use the handy copy button to copy Scenario 1 to Scenario 3, then change both of their life expectancy to 100, which is not that unusual these days. Dick had earlier not counted on long-term care, since he expected to pass at age 86. We better fix that if he's planning on 100. This is why it's very important to think additional scenarios through. Often the one "quick" thing you think you want to test has other consequences that must also be modeled.

We rename Scenario 3 to "Both live to 100" and change the long-term care expenses to $80,000 per year for each of them, starting at age 90. That's a very healthy ten years of LTC costs accounted for. Monte Carlo analysis reveals 87%, they're good to go! Remember, this could probably be pushed over the 90% mark by doing our optimization steps covered in the last chapter, which you should always do when you're serious about going with a scenario. Scenario 2 was so far off, it's not likely optimization could cover that gap. It was very much pie in the sky, after all!

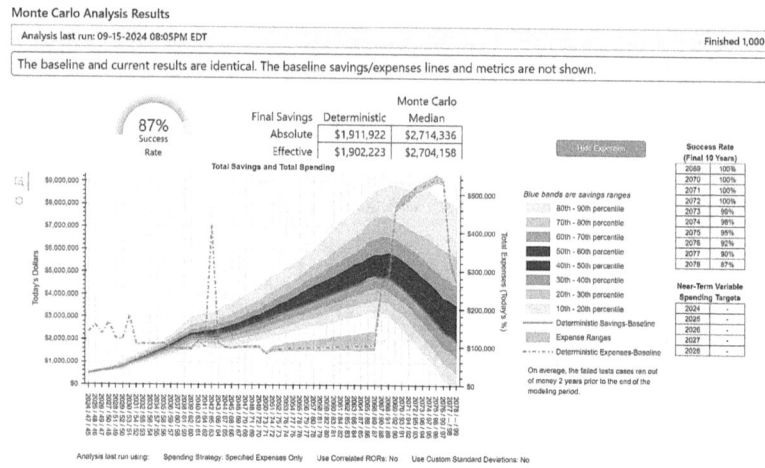

Monte Carlo Analysis Scenario 3

Now that we have three scenarios fleshed out, we can go to Analyze→Scenario Analysis Comparisons. This page presents a wonderful set of graphs that will show the differences between our scenarios right up against each other. We can easily see the raging success of Scenario 1, versus the bottom-dwelling failure of Scenario 2, versus the solid success of Scenario 3. For scenarios that might be closer in their results, it's easy to see exactly when the payoff is for one versus another. If it's very late in life, it might not be as attractive as the bottom line numbers led you to believe.

Key Baseline Metrics by Scenario

Baseline metrics are established or updated whenever the Monte Carlo -or- Historical Analysis is run. The chart will be the same for both Monte Carlo and Historical Analysis.

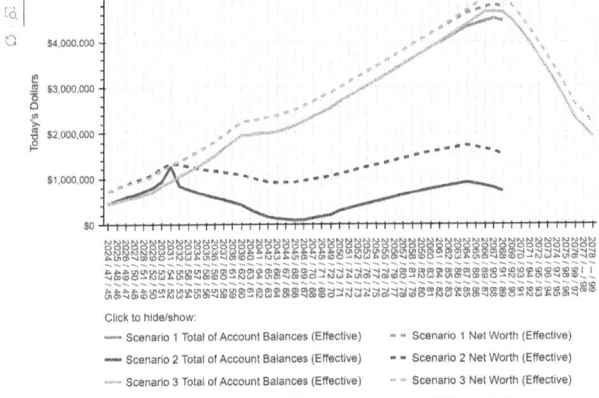

Scenario Comparison Key Metrics

10th and 90th Percentile Metrics by Scenario

This chart compares the range of final savings, between the 10th and 90th deciles, for each scenario. The metrics shown will differ depending on whether you have chosen the Monte Carlo or Historical analysis.

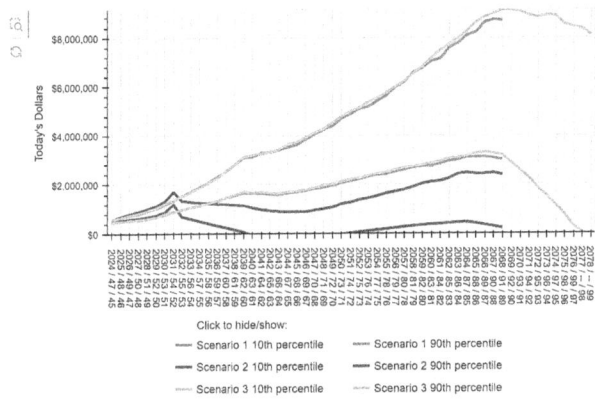

Scenario Comparison Percentiles

The scenario comparison by key metrics graph is more useful than the percentiles graph. The former will show you the differences in account balances and net worth over time, whereas the latter shows success percentage of the three scenarios. The success percentages are also shown in a table below the graph, so it's easier to scan that and look for anything sub-optimal.

## CHAPTER ELEVEN

ROUTINE MONEY PATH MAINTENANCE

WHERE TO GO FROM HERE!

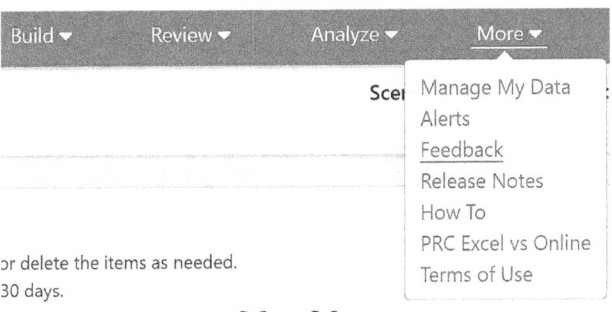

More Menu

More Menu

LET'S NOT NEGLECT THAT last, lonely menu item labeled More. It's got a bunch of very important housekeeping stuff! The first stop is More→Manage My Data, so let's head there. The first tab is Share. It allows you go grant access to the Pralana site admins, so they can help troubleshoot any issues you may run into. Remember, I'm an advocate for never putting account numbers or even your last names in the plan. It really needs nothing sensitive, other than your birth date. So, there's not much harm in this. Still, as a habit, I'd turn it on when needed, and off otherwise.

Below that, you'll see you can share your plan with an advisor or planner, like me! They would need to be registered with Pralana as an advisor, and thus granted an advisor code for you to enter here. Same drill, after doing your business with them, I'd recommend turning the sharing off. You might use this to get your plan validated with a second set of (professional) eyes after making your annual January update, or to review any new scenarios or other non-minor changes to your plan. Be wary of anyone that uses this opportunity to sell you products or services! Not that it's wrong, you may need or want those, but vet carefully as with anything important.

The next tab over, Backup, does just what it sounds like. When you're using Pralana Online, your data is stored on their servers. I recommend keeping your own backup as well (the Pralana team doesn't keep old copies, just your current one), especially if you're about to make a big change. This file is encrypted, so there's no risk of someone finding it and reading your financial info. I recommend backing up the old year's plan just prior to updating your plan in the new year, as a fallback. And, make sure your computer (or wherever you put this backup) is backed up somewhere, in case of theft, failure, etc. I love using Google Drive, because they keep versions of files for me and their security is very good. Using this feature is simple—just press the Backup My Plan button, and a save dialog should pop up. Put it somewhere safe and that you'll remember later!

TIP: I would resist the temptation to rename this plan, per the warnings on the page. Rather, put it in a descriptive folder, or create a similarly named text file wherever you put it that has notes and info about what the file represents.

The Restore tab also does just what you'd think. It will allow you to reload your plan from a backup file you created in the step above. Be careful though—you can have only one plan in the system. So, if you do this restore, whatever is loaded in Pralana Online currently will be over-written and gonzo. Like, for good! Always read the information on the screens before taking actions, it's very detailed and it's there for a reason.

The Delete tab is the nuclear bomb. Using the button on that page will cause your plan to be wiped clean from the Pralana servers. They won't be able to recover it for you! It's up to you to cover yourself by using the above facilities to back things up, as well as the other things I've mentioned throughout this book (always saving off your input, output, and tax return reports, as well as key tabular and graphical projections in PDF and/or Excel files).

The Adopt tab is pretty cool. You can also use this to transfer your plan to an advisor, but the difference is that it's not "shared," it's literally transferred over to them and gone from your profile. It's not limited to advisors, though. Suppose your super techy, cool, financially knowledgeable kids build your plan for you, and want to turn it over. You want to adopt so it's off their profile and maybe they can then start up their own plan. Or, if your planner/advisor does a plan for you, this is the way they send the final product your way and get it off their list of plans (advisor plans only allow so many active plans). Again, be careful. If you had been working on something on your end, then adopt that plan from your kids or advisor, what you had before is overlaid, and, you guessed it—gone.

To adopt, you need to get the plan code from the other person, plug that in to the field, as well as the birthdate of person one in the plan. You might think, "What's stopping them from turning right around and adopting it back away from me?" The savvy Pralana team anticipated this. The plan code will change when you adopt it, so it's no longer known by them!

Have a look back at the upper right of the Pralana page. We covered the copy feature. At times, you might see an orange circular icon with an exclamation point in it. That means there are alerts to view! Always monitor that area of the page to make sure you're in the scenario you think you are, watch for alerts here, and click that icon to investigate if you see them.

The green UM icon is for the user manual, which is incredibly well done. I always keep that open in another tab, and search it frequently. It's indexed as well, making it easy to find things. Finally, you see a Feedback link. This is your way to report any problems or suggestions to the Pralana team. You can enter bugs, usability items, feature requests, or notes about the user manual.

Financial Plan Housekeeping

That takes care of the in-app maintenance. What's left? Just basic personal finance housekeeping. During the year, monitor the balance of your cash (checking/savings) accounts. If the total exceeds what you indicated as your cash ceiling in the planning tool, transfer that to your taxable brokerage account. Over the course of the year, those transfers should reflect whatever the planning tool projected in the tabular projections. If not, your spending projection is likely off. Same thing if you have to withdraw more from your accounts than the tool projected. If you're using a cash flow monitoring/budgeting tool, pull up those end-of-year numbers and carefully compare them to what you told the tool you'd be spending.

Toward the end of each year, say, early December, take stock of your tax situation. Check your last paystubs and account statements and try to build out the beginnings of your return. Tools like dinkytown.net have useful tax tools for this, or find an advisor or planner that uses the awesome Holistiplan tool. The return should look somewhat like the tax report that Pralana generates for you. If not, track down why. If the planning tool is suggesting a Roth conversion for this year, juxtapose it with what your actual data is saying, and maybe top if off to max out whatever marginal tax bracket you'll be in. The Roth conversion, as well as things like loss and gain harvesting from your taxable brokerage and charitable giving, must be done by December 31. Don't wait until the last week, or the transaction may not go through.

> TIP: It's not uncommon for plans to be off in the first year, when doing this end-of-year checking. Hey, you're new at this, and just getting organized for maybe the first time. The planning process by nature helps us to be more knowledgeable, cognizant, and aware of our financial flow. You'll find that each subsequent year, you get better and better at it, and the results and accuracy speak to that.

If the account balances are off compared to what the planning tool said they would be, it could just be normal asset return volatility. There's no way to account for that year to year, so don't be tempted to change your projections there. It should be reflective in what you're invested in and the normal behavior of those assets, not what happened "last year" because the following year will almost certainly be different. We're modeling for the long haul!

Each January, back up your plan, save off the PDFs from the tabular and graphical projections and reports, and copy your old plan over to a new one. Update the starting year of the plan and the initial balances to your start-of-year balances, as well as anything else that's changed. When you get ready to do your taxes for real, once again compare that final return to what the planning tool has projected.

Re-run and re-optimize your analysis for the new year. If you're using a bucketing system, use the process described in Kiss Your Money Hello! (and Financial Stress Goodbye) to refill your buckets for the new year and onward using the withdrawal schedule laid out by the planning tool. Divide the amounts from each account by twelve and set up automatic transfers each month to your checking account, just like a paycheck. Don't forget to withhold some taxes from any pretax accounts. Use your projected marginal tax rate and your safe harbor rate as a guide to how much. If you have inherited IRAs, make sure you understand the requirements on those.

Lastly, have a sit-down with your spouse or partner if you have one, and go over everything with them. They should understand the mechanics as well, even if at a high level. You may be the financial driver in the family, but fate can be funny (or horrible). You don't want someone you love to be thrown to the predatory wolves in this business. That's another key reason to keep it simple, as well as protecting yourself from very expensive DIY mistakes as you age.

Monitor the Pralana user forum. It's full of great tricks and hacks, and a good way to get your questions answered. Keep an eye on the More→Release Notes menu as new features are released, and take advantage of those by incorporating them into your plan. As of this writing, these are on the menu:

- Mid-year account growth: Allows the tool to more accurately project account balances when there's activity throughout the year.

- Same-year taxation on unscheduled withdrawals: We discussed this Chapter 4. Fixes a circular reference problem with same-year taxing on unscheduled withdrawals. A current fix is to change your unscheduled withdrawals to scheduled withdrawals when your planning is complete.

- Custom tabular projections: This will allow you to turn unwanted columns off for a more concise report.

- Term life insurance recommendations: If there are any shortfalls in the event one spouse passes away, the tool will recommend term life amounts to remedy the problem.

- Charitable Trusts: Modeling of donor-advised funds and charitable trusts that do charity bunching for tax efficiency.

- Sensitivity Analysis: Allows in-time modeling of certain parameters (Social Security claiming ages, life expectancy, inflation, etc.) without having to change your plan parameters.

Wrapping Up

So, that's all I have for ya. We kicked this book off with the dramatic story of the founder of the Pralana planning tool. It was impactful and motivational. That's where I want to leave you. Stuart talked about being able to sleep at night. That's just one benefit of having a plan. It helps resolve financial stress in relationships, which is the number one reason for breakups and divorce. It provides the assurance that you've done all you can, mathematically, to live the rest of your life on your own terms, even if that means continuing to go to a job you love.

I'm so happy you made it this far in my book! Every time I help someone just like you see the light at the end of the tunnel, show them it's not an oncoming train, and share their tears of joy, I feel like I've accomplished what I was put here to do. If I've helped you at all, I only have one ask in return. Could you head to your favorite book sites and provide a review? They make all the difference in terms of exposure and the algos.

You can do this. You've worked hard and you deserve it. Don't forget to have fun and enjoy every sandwich!

ABOUT THE AUTHOR

Bill Hines is a Master Financial Coach, Investment Advisor Representative, and Financial/Retirement/FIRE planner located in the Lehigh Valley region of Pennsylvania, USA.

He is the founder of Money Coach Group, Inc (an organization that has helped countless clients emerge from debt to a better life) and Emancipare (an organization that provides honest, ethical, inexpensive, advice-only, flat-fee, fee-only, fiduciary investment advice and financial planning).

A proud United States Air Force Veteran, he used his GI Bill benefits for a Bachelor of Science degree from New York Institute of Technology and an Associate Degree in Information Technology from Tulsa Jr College.

Originally hailing from the Garden State of New Jersey, Bill has also lived for many years in Hershey, PA (Chocolatetown, USA). He has dedicated his professional life to helping people rise up from money stress, become financially independent, invest well, avoid getting scammed and ripped off, and living their one life on their own terms, each and every day.

All books available at wildlakellc.com (buy direct!) and other major booksellers as eBook, audiobook, and paperback.

Mindful Gratitude: A Six-Month Gratitude Journal for Veterans by Derek Hines

This is my son's book. He's a US Marine combat veteran, and he designed this journal to help other veterans, but anyone can benefit from daily mindfulness and gratitude!

Personal Finance Titles by Bill Hines

Plan Your Money Path: Create Your Own Financial Plan
Plan Your Money Path contains thousands of dollars worth of professional financial planning advice, hints, tips, and hacks. It walks you through creating a financial plan using inexpensive financial planning software.

Kiss Your Money Hello (and Financial Stress Goodbye)
Your guide to a financially independent life. This book is a modern, comprehensive guide to your personal finances.
Show and Sell 2023: Selling Your Home Today, A Cautionary Tale
A hilarious guide to saving thousands of dollars marketing and selling (or buying!) your home yourself.

Recommended Fiction from Wild Lake LLC

Farawayer: A Novel (literary fiction)
"...a sweeping literary travelogue that evokes Kerouac's On the Road and Salinger's Catcher in the Rye..."
Hitchhiking and motorcycling are a means to a destination, but you can't outrun your demons.
Vigilante Angels Trilogy (noir crime)
If you were going to die, who would you kill? A dark, gritty trilogy. Buckle up and prepare to ride a roller-coaster of vigilante justice.
DroidMesh Trilogy (all-ages sci-fi, teen hero with disabilities)
Can the sorrow of a father, the challenge of a feat never accomplished, and the promise of normalcy for a son who has never known it motivate a man beyond his ethical boundaries? What happens when it all goes wrong?
Rambles and Daydreams (short stories)